Kate Daly is the founder of the award-winning separation service *amicable*, a leading divorce expert and a qualified relationship counsellor. She was an outspoken advocate for the campaign to introduce no-fault divorce in England and Wales in 2022, and is the host of *The Divorce Podcast*. *amicable divorce* is her first book.

Praise for *amicable divorce*

'A comforting, practical and deeply compassionate guide for anyone navigating the divorce process ... this book truly reflects [*amicable*'s] commitment to doing divorce differently – with humanity and care at its heart'

Emma Campbell, aka Limitless Em

'*amicable divorce* is a powerful re-imagining of what separation can look like ... It shows parents a different path, one rooted in cooperation, emotional safety and long-term emotional security for the whole family. An essential read for anyone who wants to separate with dignity, care and intention'

Catherine Morgan, founder of The Money Panel

'Clear and helpful ... [Kate Daly] deals with this topic sensitively and pragmatically'

> **Joanna Harrison, author of *Five Arguments All Couples (Need to) Have***

'Kate's book is refreshing and beautifully written ... If you have bought this excellent book, buy another one and give it to a friend – we all know someone who is separating. Be part of that change. Let's make the process of separation kinder, more accepting and less judgemental'

> **Rebecca Giraud, co-director of Only Mums & Dads**

'Important and necessary ... all told in the tone of your helpful, chatty, expert friend. It would have been profoundly useful to me when I was navigating the choppy seas of divorce myself'

> **Wendy Wason, comedian**

'Few experiences can upend your life like divorce. With rare clarity and practical wisdom, Kate Daly demystifies the process and shows how to end a marriage with integrity and self-respect while staying squarely focused on your kids'

> **Christina McGhee, author of *Parenting Apart***

amicable divorce

Your Practical Guide to Divorce Without the Drama

Kate Daly

SOUVENIR
PRESS

First published in Great Britain in 2026 by

Souvenir Press
an imprint of Profile Books Ltd
29 Cloth Fair
London
EC1A 7JQ

www.souvenirpress.co.uk

Copyright © Kate Daly, 2026

1 3 5 7 9 10 8 6 4 2

Typeset and designed by seagulls.net

Printed and bound in Great Britain by CPI Group (UK) Ltd, Croydon, CR0 4YY

This book is intended as general guidance to help readers navigate divorce more amicably. It does not constitute legal advice and responsibility for decisions made using the information remains with the reader.

The moral right of the author has been asserted.

All rights reserved. Without limiting the rights under copyright reserved above, no part of this publication may be reproduced, stored or introduced into a retrieval system, or transmitted, in any form or by any means (electronic, mechanical, photocopying, recording or otherwise), without the prior written permission of both the copyright owner and the publisher of this book.

Profile Books takes seriously the responsibility of defending our authors' copyright. No part of this book may be used or reproduced in any manner for the purpose of training artificial intelligence technologies or systems (including but not limited to machine learning models and large language models (LLMs)). In accordance with Article 4(3) of the DSM Directive 2019/790, Profile Books expressly reserves this work from the text and data mining exception.

A CIP catalogue record for this book is available from the British Library.

Our product safety representative in the EU is BGC Sustainability
& Compliance, 7 avenue du Général Leclerc, Paris, 75014, France
https://baldwinglobalconsulting.com

ISBN 978 1 80522 610 9
eISBN 978 1 80522 612 3

For Imogen and Lucas, who survived our acrimonious divorce and inspired a kinder way.

Whilst my name is on the cover of this book, the heart and soul of everyone who's been on the amicable journey is contained within, and I am grateful to each and every person.

Contents

Note to the Reader — viii

Introduction — 1

1. What's Love Got to Do With It? — 15
2. Is It Over? Should I Leave? — 35
3. The Choice Is (Y)ours — 73
4. What Is an Amicable Divorce? — 93
5. D-I-V-O-R-C-E — 125
6. The Kids Are Our Priority: Cooperative Parenting — 151
7. School Shoes and Smartphones: Who Pays for the Children? — 189
8. Money, Money, Money — 207
9. From Us to Me: Life After Love — 247

A Final Note — 281

Resources — 286
Acknowledgements — 291
Index — 292

Note to the Reader

This book provides advice for those going through separation and divorce, but it does not offer an exhaustive legal guide to divorce.

Where divorce law is discussed it refers to the law in England and Wales. Scotland and Northern Ireland are separate jurisdictions with different laws and there are links to further sources of information in the Resources section.

Please also note that, as the legal procedures and emotional challenges of divorce apply equally to marriage and civil partnership, when I use the terms 'marriage' and 'divorce', unless otherwise stated, these can also relate to civil partnership and dissolution.

Introduction

No one thinks they will get divorced. *amicable*, the company I co-founded, exists because I did get divorced – twice. So you could say I'm a bit of an expert, both personally and now professionally, having helped thousands of couples untie the knot amicably.

If I were to give you one tip to start your journey off, it's this: whatever you do, don't google 'divorce'. I'm serious. Don't ask your divorced friends, colleagues or your mum's neighbour about their experience and absolutely don't watch anything on TV about divorce. You'll be confronted with tales of betrayal, legal battles, custody wars and financial wrangling in a hellish and very public spectacle of personal failure.

Divorce certainly has a bad reputation, but does it have to? Wouldn't it be better if we changed the narrative, to see divorce not as a failure, but as a transition that can be handled with kindness and mutual respect? With nearly half of all marriages ending in divorce in the UK, it's surely time to rethink how we approach it.

If you make the extremely hard decision to separate or end your marriage – or if that decision is made for you – you haven't 'failed' and you're not a 'bad person'. You're human. And like all humans, you're trying to find happiness and a contented life for you and your family.

Make no mistake – for many, the ending of a marriage is a deeply sad experience. I know how emotionally gruelling it can be, and how easy it is to become trapped in a cycle of escalating conflict and mounting costs. Scarred by the process and still living with the consequences of my second divorce over a decade later, I became determined to develop a different, more compassionate way to divorce, one that puts people and families, rather than legal battles, at its heart. The system that I went on to develop – and which I share in this book – has helped a huge number of couples, whether amicable is a reality or an aspiration, to end their relationships amicably and with kindness.

Creating *amicable* was very much a personal mission, my goal to save other people from the emotional mincing machine I had been through, with lawyers pitted against each other, chewing me up and spitting me out the other side. I hate that there is a section within an industry that profits from conflict and division, especially when it comes to families, and many lawyers and legal minds feel the same way. To be clear, it's not lawyers individually who are always the problem; it's often the system and the lens through which they look.

introduction

For too long, divorce and separation have been approached as a purely legal matter, in a system that is by its nature adversarial, forcing those funnelled into it to take sides in a conflict. While this may work in criminal law, the unintended consequence in family law is that it pits spouse against spouse, parent against parent, and creates discord and friction that can have life-long consequences.

That said, my experience of divorce hadn't been all bad: in fact, my first divorce was similar to the kind of amicable separation I now help couples achieve. Our circumstances helped: we were in our late twenties, without children, and our only shared asset was a first home we had bought together. There was sadness because our once loving relationship had ended, not due to any major drama but because our careers and lives had been pulling in different directions, and in hindsight we perhaps shouldn't have married. For me at least, there was less of a sense of upset and distress and more a desire to correct a mistake in a way that was dignified and respectful.

Neither of us wanted or felt we needed to spend lots of money on a divorce – and looking back we were certainly right in that decision. We ended up using a lawyer we knew, who despite not being a divorce specialist was happy to do the paperwork. We were keen to keep things simple, but it still felt as though there were a lot of hoops to jump through, and we were both shocked to learn that we couldn't use a single lawyer to draft our agreement on behalf of both of us. So only I instructed the lawyer, and we negotiated our financial agreement ourselves.

My second divorce was entirely different. We lawyered up and found ourselves in an endless legal battle and a whole heap of pain, frustration and crippling expense. My circumstances by then were very different as I was in my thirties and had given up work to care for our two children, then both under the age of three. A whirlwind romance had led to a marriage that quickly began to fall apart, although for a long time I pretended it wasn't happening and that I could manage the situation. I couldn't, and it reached a point where I realised it was going to be dangerous for me and the children to stay.

On leaving, I felt completely at a loss, and with no income of my own I couldn't imagine how I could pay for any legal help until a financial advisor recommended that I cash in an ISA to cover the costs. When I then explained my situation to a solicitor, and the assets at stake, I could sense straight away that I was being evaluated not as the emotionally raw and vulnerable person I was but as a legal case, and a lucrative one at that.

My ex had also engaged lawyers and, before we knew it, we were caught in a system driven by two warring sides battling to the bitter end at our own expense and leaving us utterly decimated. Whenever I saw an email from my lawyer, let alone one from the 'other side', I felt physically sick. I came to regard Form E, the dreaded document for which you must locate, list and provide evidence for every financial asset you have, as the miserable love child of a psychopath and an accountant. It meant tracking down all our bank statements, payslips, pension contributions, premium bonds, sales receipts – everything. Having just gone back to work, I had to take a week off to complete the form, which still wasn't enough. The whole experience reduced me to tears.

At a time when cooperation, understanding and communication were the most precious commodities, we were separated and siloed with our lawyers. Every time I wanted to talk to my solicitor, or get them to read a document, I was charged. I was being ripped apart financially and emotionally, and yet I hardly dared contact the very person meant to help and protect me for fear that legal costs would eat away at the money I would need to rebuild my life and that of our children.

We ended up in full-blown court proceedings for both the finances and arrangements for the children, all of which fuelled a billing frenzy from our respective legal teams. Many times my friends had to scrape me off the floor. They looked after the kids when I had to trek into town to see my lawyer and bought me a hole punch and stapler (and wine!) when the need to save costs by putting together my own legal bundles became an imperative.

It felt like just a hop, skip and a jump – one or two phone calls, and emotionally charged decisions – before we found ourselves embroiled in a full final hearing. For the uninitiated that's three separate court hearings, solicitor and barrister fees for each one, plus all the costs in between.

The process took nearly two years and cost me a huge amount financially and psychologically, placing an almost unbearable stress on my day-to-day life. It doesn't surprise me now to learn that divorce ranks as more stressful and more likely to cause health problems because of this stress than major illness or incarceration, second only to the death of a spouse or a child. Why is this the case? Why does a divorce have to be so psychologically harmful, and is there a way of reducing and minimising the stress of separation?

During the divorce I knew I had to get back to work – against the advice of lawyers, I might add, who argued it would be better for my case if I didn't. But for my own sanity and security it was something I needed to do. With a master's degree in counselling and psychology, along with experience in business, I set up a counselling practice specialising in relationship breakdown.

As part of that work, I briefly joined some local solicitors involved in a collaborative pod, where lawyers, psychologists and financial experts work together to help clients make better decisions during the divorce process. I thought it was an admirable scheme but I also felt it was quite an expensive service and unaffordable for most people.

The problem largely stemmed from the fact that lawyers rarely work on a fixed-fee basis, preferring instead to bill in six-minute intervals and invoice as they go along. This only adds to the financial strain and emotional anxiety of the process, and so I began to explore whether I could start a business offering a more accessible service for couples.

Fixed fees were key, as was a focus on the emotional journey of divorce, alongside the financial and legal consequences. I felt that if we worked with couples together from the outset – rather than as individuals pitted against each other – we could achieve better outcomes for everyone involved.

I discussed the idea with my friend Pip, who had given me a lot of support during my second divorce, and she thought it was brilliant. With a background in technology, she knew that tech would act as a catalyst for the business and allow us to scale. With our very different backgrounds we made a good pairing, and in 2015 we began to set up what became *amicable*.

Thereafter we began to finesse the kind of service we would offer. Our goal was always to begin with the emotional journey and to assess from the outset how emotionally ready couples were to work through the divorce process. If someone is feeling defensive and fearful then they're going to push back on decisions, so we felt we needed to create a safe space for couples to unpack their feelings so they could move on.

By looking at everything through the lens of emotion we could then tackle the legal process and the financial outcome, making sure that both partners had somewhere to live, enough money to live on from day to day, and savings for retirement.

In order to devise a framework for our service, I grabbed some large sheets of paper and went back to the basics, mapping out the emotional journey of divorce based on my own experience and my master's degree research. The mapping took into account the two very emotional journeys of separation: the one you're on if you're the instigator, and the other, very different, journey if you're receiving the news.

I then mapped onto the emotional journey the legal process of divorce, the tasks we have to achieve, along with the financial objectives for each spouse. I encouraged couples to focus on their long-term goals – parenting and family life being a priority, alongside financial objectives – and ultimately the model we set up proved hugely successful, with 95 per cent of customers who start the *amicable* process achieving a legally binding financial agreement approved by the court.

So, we have built a business that has people, instead of the law, at its heart. We inject kindness into the process, and we have changed the legal landscape by working with couples rather than individuals and by helping them negotiate financial settlements together rather than having to seek separate legal advice. We prioritised the family as a whole and deconstructed the idea of sides, of winners and losers. From the off, it was clear we had built something customers wanted.

What has been more challenging, however, is navigating just how upset the traditional legal industry and the judiciary would be. In 2019, we were summoned to the High Court to defend our idea of working for couples, specifically whether we could legally draft consent orders – the legal documents that set out the financial arrangements as part of a divorce. As I discovered in my first divorce, a firm of solicitors generally cannot represent both sides in a dispute. As we are not solicitors, we challenged those rules, arguing that they did not apply to us, and that if we had the formal agreement of both partners they would not be conflicted in using the *amicable* service. It was perhaps one of the most difficult times for us as a business. As I wasn't sent to prison (the penalty if we had lost would have been two years' jail time!), you can surmise that we won our court case. In summing up, the judge praised us for providing 'access to justice for many people effectively disenfranchised from the legal process' and commended our services as having a 'clear social benefit'.

Our High Court victory showed that just because it's always been done a certain way doesn't mean it has to stay the same forever, and consumer demand can force change to happen. The *amicable* method has proven to be a real game changer and I'm immensely proud to have helped so many couples separate in a kinder and better way. The benefits are immeasurable, not least in that it significantly limits the impact of divorce on children, both in the short and long term, while helping people move on to whatever they want to do next.

In this book I will reveal our tried-and-tested methods and how to achieve an amicable divorce or separation, without conflict or relying on lawyers. If you and your partner simply want to go your separate ways, but you want to do so kindly and with the minimum of stress, then this book is for you. If you want to continue to co-parent your children or make joint decisions about your future, keep reading. If an amicable divorce currently feels like a distant aspiration – perhaps because communication with your partner is strained – I can help you turn that aspiration into reality. And even if you have already started to go down the traditional solicitor route, many of the techniques and methods will ease the process. Inside you'll find practical tools, guidance and real-life strategies to support you as you navigate the next steps.

We'll explore the emotional journey of divorce, because whatever you're feeling now, you're not alone. I'll share tips on building resilience and taking care of your mental and emotional well-being. You'll learn how to communicate with your partner, reduce tension and avoid any unnecessary conflict. I'll guide you through creating an effective and workable parenting plan that puts the needs of your children first, as well as how to agree on finances and how to work through any potential disagreements.

The book will also provide tips for life after divorce: how to take the opportunity to re-evaluate, move on and feel positive about the future. I have collated insights and takeaways from our divorce specialists and cooperative parenting coaches as well as from real-life case studies of couples who have faced similar challenges and found a way to separate amicably. Their stories are illuminating, sometimes heart-rending, but ultimately inspiring.

I'll also cover the legal and financial aspects of divorce and separation, which are relevant whether you're using a service like *amicable* or working with solicitors, and whether you're married, in a civil partnership or cohabiting. The legal content is focused on England and Wales, but the emotional journey and how to be a cooperative parent are universal concepts and can be applied wherever you live.

My aim with the book is to change the narrative around divorce and separation and to show how unnecessary it is for many couples to go down the warring solicitor route, which can so easily escalate into further conflict and division. I have been there and I know how damaging it is. At times, it felt like being swept into a fast-moving river, suddenly submerged and tossed from one side to the other, until you're dumped out into the open sea, bruised and fighting to breathe.

But it doesn't have to be that way, and I want to offer a different experience. The journey doesn't have to be a torrent but can instead be more of a gentle chalk stream, with calmer waters and places to pause before continuing on your way.

If that sounds like the kind of divorce or separation you want – or hope to work towards – then read on. You're not alone – I've been there too and know the pain and uncertainty that comes with this life change. But I also know that, with the right support, divorce doesn't have to destroy but can be a moment of transformation. Together we can reshape how divorce is done and create a more positive path for those who follow.

1

What's Love Got to Do With It?

Love and marriage may go together like a horse and carriage, so says the song – but only very recently, and the carriage has changed – a lot. Throughout much of history, marriage was a strategic arrangement designed to consolidate wealth or cement family ties. Love, if it existed between spouses at all, was often considered a 'fortunate by-product' rather than a prerequisite, and for most ordinary people divorce was simply not an option: you either stayed together, informally separated or – as was often the case – one of you died and the other remarried.

By the Middle Ages, religion played a central role in formalising marriage, defined by the Christian Church as a sacred union sanctioned by God. This spiritual framing helped reinforce the permanence and indissolubility of marriage – much to the annoyance of perhaps England's most famous divorcee, King Henry VIII – and divorce became not only legally difficult but morally condemned. In contrast, other traditions – such as in Islamic cultures – allowed for divorce, though often within strict gendered rules.

Subsequent centuries saw a greater emphasis on individual rights, autonomy and personal happiness, and love gradually moved to the forefront of marital expectations, along with personal fulfilment. These cultural shifts combined with industry and a burgeoning of the cities, and with less dependence on land and inheritance, we gained more freedom to choose our partners.

By the early twentieth century divorce, rather than death, had become the most common way an unhappy relationship might come to an end, and had grown accessible to a broader range of people beyond just the very wealthy. Divorce laws and social attitudes, however, were still heavily biased in favour of men, and it wasn't until the Matrimonial Causes Act of 1923 that women could petition for divorce on the same grounds as men. Before this, under the Act's 1857 predecessor, a man could divorce his wife solely on the grounds of adultery whereas a woman had to prove adultery *plus* an additional offence like cruelty or desertion.

With limited access to employment, women continued to face severe financial hardship following divorce and the social stigma left them isolated and economically vulnerable. Men were also more likely to gain custody of children, especially in the earlier part of the twentieth century when fathers were legally seen as the rightful guardians. This slowly shifted over time, particularly by the 1920s and 1930s, when mothers were increasingly seen as the primary caregivers for young children. The shame of divorce, however, led many women to stay in unhappy relationships for fear of being labelled 'damaged goods'. Those who went ahead with it could find themselves shunned in society or even publicly disgraced in the newspapers, which thrived on the scandal and drama of divorce cases.

The stigma surrounding divorce in turn led to a fault-based legal system, in which one spouse had to prove the other was at 'fault' – through misconduct or moral transgression – for the court to grant a divorce. In the 1920s, the main fault accepted by the courts was still adultery, forcing some couples to fabricate scenarios to meet the narrow legal requirements, typically a husband checking into a hotel to be 'accidentally' discovered with a paid companion.

Over the subsequent decades other faults or 'grounds' like cruelty, desertion and unreasonable behaviour were added, and this eventually led to the five-fault divorce system that remained in place right through to 2022. This meant that couples, unless they were already separated, had to accuse each other of being at fault, which amped up the conflict and made an already difficult process more adversarial and emotionally charged. Thankfully, by the twenty-first century, England and Wales had caught up with the rest of the Western world and introduced 'no-fault divorce'. This means that couples no longer need to assign blame or provide evidence of wrongdoing. They simply state that the marriage has irretrievably broken down – no public airing of moral failings or courtroom drama required.

Changes in divorce laws over time both reflected and helped to shift public perception around divorce, which no longer carries as heavy a stigma as it once did. In general, we see divorce as a personal choice or a life transition and not as a shameful or shocking event. With more than four out of ten marriages in the UK now ending in divorce, we don't expect people to tough it out in toxic relationships over the course of our now much longer lives.

Attitudes about marriage have also shifted considerably and there is far less pressure on couples to marry if they live together or have children. Yet marriage remains popular – according to the Office for National Statistics, in 2023 married couples still made up about two-thirds of family households. At the same time, cohabitation – that is, living together without having walked down the aisle – is on the rise, and roughly 22 per cent of adults in the UK who live together cohabit. Some may go on to marry or enter into a civil partnership, but many are happy as they are, although cohabiting couples have far less legal protection than married or civil-partnered couples, a situation that legal reforms may soon address.

Official marriage statistics of course now include same-sex couples, who gained the right to marry in England and Wales in March 2014. Since then, thousands of same-sex couples have chosen to tie the knot, rising from 26,000 in 2015 to a total of 167,000 by 2022. Civil partnerships, originally introduced for same-sex couples in 2004, were extended to opposite-sex couples in December 2019, offering more options when it comes to formalising relationships.

While marriages are still far more prevalent than civil partnerships by about 35 to 1, they both provide similar legal rights, and any differences are primarily in symbolic meaning and procedure, such as the fact that civil partnership ceremonies are only secular, whereas marriage ceremonies can be religious or secular. Terminology also differs between the two – marriages are ended through divorce and civil partnerships through dissolution – although the legal processes are largely the same. Note that when I use the terms 'marriage' and 'divorce' throughout the book, unless otherwise stated, it can also relate to civil partnership and dissolution. The legal procedures and the emotional challenges of divorce apply equally to dissolution.

While couples choose to divorce at all ages – the average marriage length in 2023 for opposite-sex couples was around twelve and a half years – there has been an increasing trend for older couples to divorce. In 2021 almost one in four divorces were granted to couples over the age of 50, including retirees or couples who had been married for as long as thirty or forty years. Looking at what has led to this increase can shed light also on a few other general trends when it comes to marriage, relationships and divorce:

- We're living longer. Fifty years ago, the average life expectancy for a man was 69 and a woman 75.

Today it's 84 for men and 87 for women, and many live well into their nineties. With more years ahead of them, as people age or retire, they want to enjoy the next chapter of their lives without being tied down in a marriage that no longer brings them happiness. Many are in good health, and have no plans to slow down or settle for a life of quiet dissatisfaction.

- Women are more independent and less financially reliant on their partners, and after divorce they don't necessarily rush into another marriage. Men over the age of 55 are twice as likely to remarry than women in the same age bracket, suggesting that many women are content to remain on their own. For men, remarrying seems to improve their health – a study in Norway covering ages 40 to 89, from 1970–2008, found that men who remarried within ten years of divorce or widowhood had mortality rates on a par with men whose first marriage never ended. Remarriage for women, however, didn't reduce their mortality risk to the same levels as first-time married women and it seems the health benefits are less clear-cut.
- Once children have flown the nest, the focus shifts back onto parents and sometimes couples discover they are no longer as connected as they once were. With fewer distractions, long-standing tensions or unacceptable behaviour – whether it's minor domestic disputes or extramarital affairs – can become harder to ignore.

~ Growing older often brings perspective, self-confidence and greater clarity about what you want from life. Television presenter Ruth Langsford said as much after her divorce, in that she felt ready to embrace being single again in the lead-up to her sixty-fifth birthday, to 'make choices that are just about me'.

While divorce later in life is on the rise, those who divorce younger may experience a different kind of awakening. Actor and director Olivia Wilde, who got divorced at the age of 27, put it this way: 'The good thing about getting divorced young – if there is a good thing – is that it makes you realise there's no schedule in life. It blasts you wide open and frees you to be honest with yourself.'

While divorces across all age groups peaked in 1993, more people now choose to cohabit – a more unstable type of relationship – which means more people are separating rather than divorcing. People separate for many reasons – often because their relationship has simply run its course – and there is far less judgement when they do. In fact, over a long life, it's not unusual to have two, three or more long relationships and few people think less of you for it.

Divorce is no longer the taboo that it once was but stigma is still felt in some communities, particularly where religion has a dominant influence. Irish actor and writer Sharon Horgan, who divorced in her late forties, remarked: 'I feel like, especially if you come from a religious background – I was brought up Catholic – divorce is kind of a dirty word. But it shouldn't be. Divorce can be a really helpful, handy thing that can change your life. There's a lot of shame attached to the failure of a relationship, and that shouldn't be the case.'

While attitudes to divorce may have softened more generally, it's not uncommon to experience a sense of personal shame or failure when a marriage ends. The expectation we have of ourselves and our hopes for the future have unravelled, leading us to view the end of a relationship as a reflection of our own inadequacy or failure. That is a common sensation, and certainly how I felt, but there are ways to combat these feelings, as I'll explain later in the book.

I've been especially interested to hear about the additional burden experienced by couples in same-sex marriages. In the podcast I record, *The Divorce Podcast*, I've listened as guests have shared their sense of shame and how they somehow have failed to honour a right that the gay community fought for decades to establish.

The broadcaster Paul Roseby explained the sense of guilt he felt after his same-sex marriage ended: 'I didn't know any other gay couple that were divorced or getting divorced. Combined with this, I didn't ever imagine that I, as a gay man, would get married because legally you weren't allowed to ... I felt completely and utterly guilty. I felt I'd failed ... I felt I'd let myself down, my friends, and my family. I felt guilt all the way.' Similarly, comedian and writer Candice Gallimore wrote of her gay divorce: 'I felt like I'd let the queer community down ... any wrong move is a chalk mark in the "cons" column for the rights of LGBTQI+ people and there feels like no bigger con mark than a failed marriage.'

There is of course a myriad of reasons why marriages end, but one of the most common – and least talked about – is the simple fact that people change. Over time, our values, goals and priorities can shift, and unless a couple is consciously working to stay connected and aligned, it's easy to find themselves moving in different directions. What begins as a shared path can quietly become two parallel lives, and many relationships suffer from what might be called relationship fatigue. Life gets busy. Careers, parenting, financial pressures, health issues – all of it takes a toll.

Amid the demands of modern life, very few people are taught or encouraged to actively maintain their relationship health in the same way we're encouraged to stay physically fit. We take courses, seek advice, and invest time and money in our professional development or physical wellness, yet when it comes to emotional connection and relational skills, many of us are simply expected to 'just know' how to make it work.

But relationships require effort – not in moments of crisis, but as a continual practice. When that effort isn't made, resentment can quietly build. Communication falters. Affection fades. The distance between two people becomes not dramatic, but habitual. And often, by the time both notice just how far apart they've grown, it feels too late to bridge the gap.

This isn't about blame. It's about understanding the nature of long-term relationships. Sometimes we get lucky in choosing the right life partner, sometimes not – and if not, we might have a good few years of marriage before we end things, or perhaps we realise early on we've made a mistake. That's okay; our lives can take us in different directions – I know mine did in my early thirties – and this might mean ending a relationship so you can move on with the next stage of your life, in which case separation can be a healthy, even necessary, choice.

Case study: Young love

Here one of our amicable divorce specialists tells her personal story of how her marriage ended. Having grown up in South Africa, she and her partner moved to the UK in their twenties. They later decided to end the marriage and managed to do so amicably.

I met my partner at high school, and it was the classic first-love and opposites-attract kind of relationship. We were deeply in love, and I thought he was the right person for me. There were communication challenges but of course when you're young you feel as though you can conquer anything. You can't see your life being any other way. We were opposites and in hindsight weren't as complementary as I thought. Perhaps if we'd been more mature in our approach or worked on our personal growth, we could have made it work.

We moved to the UK just before the pandemic and ended up living in a tiny one-bedroom flat. Working from home in a close environment and not being as social as we would have liked caused quite a lot of friction and a building-up of resentment.

We eventually decided that the relationship wasn't working anymore, after which he moved out promptly. I'm really grateful we avoided that living-together dynamic which I know can be really challenging when you're separating.

In researching the best way to divorce we looked at various options but in the end we did it ourselves in a typical kitchen-table agreement. We owned a home together, had investments and savings accounts, two vehicles and a dog, so we had started to establish important aspects of our life. Uncoupling all of that was really challenging and in the process I learned a lot about financial literacy. He was the higher-income earner, so had more oversight of finances, but he was helpful from the outset and even created a spreadsheet for me where I could put in my financial goals and salary, and it's something I still use to this day, a year and a half later!

> I don't have any regrets from the experience and there have been valuable life lessons. I've learned a lot about myself, the things I value and which personality types might gel better with my own – and how challenging the financial aspect of divorce can be.
>
> I'm still very close with his family and we have respectful boundaries, having not pursued a friendship because of the dynamics involved, and I'm certainly grateful for the outcome. Ending a relationship with someone you loved, deeply cared about and planned a life with should be amicable – and I'm so glad it was for me.

Heady with love and excitement, we might rush into marriage without fully considering the legal and financial implications of what we are doing, all of which must be unravelled if we decide to separate or divorce. Many are unaware that, when you marry, the law assumes that property, savings, pensions and debt acquired during the marriage are jointly owned, regardless of who earned or bought them. This means that if you divorce or formally separate, the starting point for dividing assets is usually a 50/50 split. (Individual need and circumstances will influence how assets are ultimately divided – a topic covered in more detail in Chapter 7.)

> ## What if you're not married?
>
> For couples who are not married or in a formal partnership, legal rights are far more limited. A frequent misconception is that, after living together for a period of time, you automatically become a 'common law' wife or husband and have similar legal rights. To be clear, there is no such thing as a common law marriage, wife or husband – no such status exists in English and Welsh law. If you haven't been through a marriage or civil partnership ceremony and do not have the relevant certificate, you are not married.
>
> This can come as quite a shock to partners coming out of long-term relationships when they discover they have no automatic rights to property, spousal support or inheritance, unless specified in their partner's will. There is currently cross-party support in government to reform the law, which would address the long-standing legal gap in the UK that currently leaves around 3.6 million couples – and women in particular – in the UK vulnerable.

One of the most seismic changes to divorce law in England and Wales came into effect with the introduction of no-fault divorce on 6 April 2022, under the Divorce, Dissolution and Separation Act. It marked an historic shift in the law following decades of campaigning by divorce and legal professionals in favour of modernising the divorce process in England and Wales and removing the need for spouses to 'blame' each other in divorce proceedings. I certainly whooped with joy when it finally passed into law, reflecting how different my own divorce might have been had it started off on a less combative note. Since setting up *amicable*, I had long been campaigning with my co-founder Pip for no-fault divorce so it's also a source of great pride that we played our part in such a transformative change in the law.

Let's go over the workings of the old divorce system and how it has changed. As you navigate your divorce journey you might come across outdated material online as well as some of the older terminology that still persists.

Up until April 2022, to get divorced in England and Wales you had to choose one of 'five facts' or reasons to prove your marriage or civil partnership had broken down irretrievably. Often referred to as grounds for divorce, these were:

- Adultery
- Unreasonable behaviour
- Two years' separation (if you both agreed)
- Five years' separation (if only one of you agreed)
- Desertion

On 6 April 2022 the law changed and no-fault divorce replaced the fault-based system above. This means you no longer need to blame each other or give *reasons to prove* that your marriage has irretrievably broken down. Instead, you make a simple statement that it has, and one of you applies for a divorce – or, *for the first time*, both of you can do this and apply for a divorce jointly.

Let's consider the key changes and how a divorce today might differ from those before April 2022.

- The new laws end the necessity for couples to blame each other or be separated for long periods of time.
- The irretrievable breakdown of the marriage is now the sole reason for divorce and replaces the five options that used to be listed on the legal documents (you cannot have a fault-based divorce – even if you want one!)
- You can now apply for a divorce or dissolve your civil partnership as an individual or as a couple.
- There is no longer an option to contest the divorce. If one of you knows it's over, it is. (The only exceptions to this are: you are not married; you are already divorced; or you think you should be divorcing in a different country.)
- There are still two stages after applying for a divorce, called the conditional order (previously called the decree nisi) and the final order (previously called the decree absolute. Another archaic term, 'divorce petition', is now 'divorce application').
- Every couple has to go through the 'twenty-week reflection period' after submitting their divorce application.

This new way of working means that couples can start their divorce off on the right footing. More people have the possibility of an amicable divorce and no longer need to place blame on each other. This means the focus can be on protecting any children without the demonisation of either parent. This is so important and crucial in setting the tone for how things should proceed. When we started, it felt odd to be encouraging couples to be amicable, only then to take them through legal paperwork that was anything but amicable. Now at least I feel our jurisdiction has caught up with the founding principles of the *amicable* system – and this feels like an important achievement!

Safety first

It's important to note that sometimes an amicable divorce is not possible. While I'd love everyone to be able to work as a couple, for some of us that's not attainable, and our safety (and that of any children) has to come first. If there's real risk of harm or coercive control in your relationship, then a more traditional legal route may be necessary as it offers protections such as court orders and other people to negotiate on your behalf.

It's important to remember abuse is not just physical; it can be psychological or financial too. So, if you are worried you are being abused, think carefully about

> the process you'll use to sort things out. It can feel disappointing or infuriating to know certain routes are closed to you, but working closely and directly with a perpetrator is dangerous and I know from experience that, no matter how 'able' or willing you are, it seldom works. See the Resources section for agencies and charities that can provide support and advice.

In summary

- For much of modern history, divorce was relatively rare and deemed shameful. That stigma resulted in a fault-based system in which one spouse had to prove the other spouse was 'at fault'.
- Attitudes about divorce have shifted considerably. We now live much longer and people who divorce are no longer ostracised in society.
- Many more couples are cohabiting or entering into civil partnerships, and since 2014 same-sex couples gained the right to marry.
- The no-fault divorce system came into effect on 6 April 2022, marking a major shift in procedure and law in England and Wales.
- The new law enables far more couples to work together, communicate, and divorce or separate amicably. You can too!

2

Is It Over? Should I Leave?

The decision to end a marriage or relationship might be the hardest one you'll ever make. It was for me – both times – and not a decision I came to overnight, but one I agonised over for many months and, in my second divorce, years. Divorce is often described in terms of grief, comparable to a bereavement. Both involve a deep sense of loss, emotional upheaval and a period of adjustment, and choosing to put yourself and your partner through all of that is rarely easy.

Divorce is rarely the result of a single dramatic event – although that can certainly happen, such as when a partner admits to adultery. More often, when I am speaking to people, it seems it stems from a gradual erosion of a relationship over time. As connection fades or unresolved tensions build, a relationship can slowly unravel, and recognising when it has truly broken down can be incredibly difficult. During the process, feelings and emotions can seesaw – the path towards separation is rarely linear – and accepting the reality that a relationship is at an end, and that you need to walk away, takes courage. That feeling of not knowing whether this is 'just how marriage is' or if it's truly broken is exhausting and lonely. My aim in this chapter is to help you decipher whether your marriage needs work or whether it's over.

Whichever stage you are at – whether you are yet to decide your relationship has run its course or if you have just learned of your partner's decision to leave – emotions will be running high. It's also likely – and this is a critical point – that you and your partner will be in very different places emotionally. Major life changes, such as grief and the breakdown of a relationship, can trigger a range of feelings and responses, as illustrated in the diagram below.

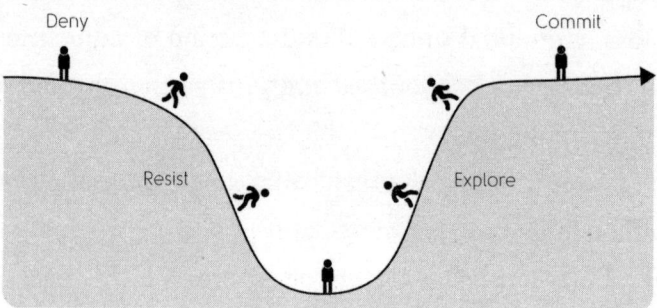

This shows the typical emotions couples go through when they are separating or divorcing and it's a useful visual reference for every stage of the process. (The curve is based on the well-known Kübler-Ross model which outlines the emotions people often experience when dealing with many kinds of loss.) The difference with divorce is that often one partner takes the lead, initiating and driving the process forward, whereas the other partner is left to react, a recipient of a decision they didn't necessarily choose. For that reason, the instigator is likely to be way ahead of the other in emotional terms and at a very different place on that curve. And even if you make a joint decision to separate, the chances of you being in the same place on the emotional curve are very slim as people adjust to change or loss at different rates.

Let's look at the various stages shown on the curve. When we are confronted by major change, especially if it's unexpected, our first instinct can be to pretend it's not happening, to go into a form of denial. Denial can manifest as anger or shame. It's a very active phase where people express their emotions. Then you move down the emotional curve into quite fierce resistance, often characterised by a lack of action, before, as time goes on, you move along the bottom of the curve and you start to explore what the new scenario will look like. You then come up the other side and begin to commit to your new way of life or changed situation.

If you are ruminating over whether to leave a relationship, you may already have gone through at least a couple of stages of that curve. Perhaps two or three years before, you were in denial that anything was wrong with the relationship and, despite your creeping doubts, you resisted doing anything about it – no marriage is perfect, right? But if you're now considering articulating to your partner that the relationship is over, then you're at least in the explore phase, if not the commit point, because you're potentially voicing this as an action you are going to take, which is a major milestone.

If, however, you are the other person, hearing for the first time that your partner wants to separate or divorce, you may be right back at the denial stage. 'What are you talking about? We're fine.' And that's before you start resisting the whole idea of separating – and the more the other person pushes the more you dig your heels in. You are on opposite sides of the emotional curve and yet the instigator is ready to discuss the next stage, wanting the other person to hurry up and get over the earth-shattering news they've just delivered.

When I speak to people, I often hear the complaint that their partner just isn't doing anything and won't engage. When I ask the person how long it's been since they told their partner they want to separate I'm still surprised to hear people say things like, 'Well, it was at least three weeks ago', which, given their entire world may just have been upended, is hardly any time at all.

The recipient of your news, who might be feeling like they've just been hit by an emotional freight train, may well not be in the right headspace to calmly explore next steps and brainstorm life plans. Instead, they need to get to grips with what you've just announced, probably by going through the denial and resistance stages, plus a host of other emotions. Only then do you have a chance of having a reasonable conversation about the next steps, exploring ideas and options for a separation. You need to give them a chance to move along that emotional curve, which takes time. How you cope in the interim and the challenges you may face along the way are all covered later in the chapter.

Deciding that a relationship has ended is one thing, of course, but choosing to leave is quite a different proposition – one doesn't necessarily lead to the other. Many people continue in an unhappy relationship either because they've convinced themselves all is well in a kind of never-ending denial phase or in the full knowledge that the relationship has failed but they're not prepared to leave it.

People stay in bad relationships because they have acclimatised to them. Sometimes we chastise ourselves for staying too long or wasting our lives but it can be hard to see what's bad when you're in it. I equate this to the boiling frog metaphor. If you drop a frog into a pan of boiling water, it will jump straight out. But if you put the frog into the pan and slowly heat up the water it will boil to death. Relationships can be hard to leave!

There are many reasons why you might choose to stay in a broken relationship. Some of the most common are:

- **Stigma** – the stigma of divorce still causes some of us to fear judgement or shame from our family, friends or community. Certain cultures and religions deem it

unacceptable to divorce, and you might fear a loss of status and identity following divorce or separation.
- **Finances** – maybe you are worried about how you will cope financially if you leave. If you're in a weaker financial position than your partner, you might not be able to imagine yourself as financially independent, or you might worry about losing shared assets, your home or your overall quality of life. The legal fees associated with divorce and the expense of starting over can also be a major deterrent.
- **Children and family** – perhaps you believe that it's better to stay in an unhappy relationship to keep the family unit together and for the sake of your children. The cultural norm has it that children benefit from a two-parent household, which might put pressure on you to stay with your partner, even when your relationship is harmful or beyond repair. You might also be extremely fearful of not seeing your children or of losing your relationship with them or 'custody' of them. (Note: 'custody' is no longer a term or concept used in English and Welsh law – see page 158 for further information.)
- **Inertia or habit** – apathy or fear of the unknown might cause you to stay in an unhappy relationship. It's easier to stick with what you know, however dysfunctional your relationship might be, perhaps because you fear loneliness, have a confused loyalty to your partner

or the way of life you have chosen, or you think it unrealistic to expect your marriage to be happy.

- **Coercive control or abuse** – if you are in an abusive or controlling relationship you may feel emotionally, psychologically or physically unable to leave. Abusers often use tactics such as manipulation, isolation, intimidation and surveillance to erode their partner's confidence and sense of autonomy. Over time, this can create a deep sense of dependency, fear and confusion. Survivors and victims of abuse may worry about being followed or punished for leaving, or may not even recognise the behaviour as abuse. This dynamic can make the idea of leaving seem not only overwhelming but also dangerous. If you recognise this issue, it's best to speak to a domestic abuse helpline or advisors (see the Resources section) and make a plan to leave safely.

How do you know if a relationship is over?

The breakdown of a relationship often involves a jumble of contradictory emotions that some couples can get trapped in without ever fully resolving. Feelings and emotions can fluctuate widely; one day you might have resolved in your mind to leave, the next there's a reconciliation. Throw in children, busy work lives and financial issues and it's no wonder you feel confused, overwhelmed and incapable of making such a momentous decision.

How can you tell if you're simply going through a 'bad patch' or your relationship has irretrievably broken down? How do you know when you've passed the point of no return? Confusingly it's quite normal for partners to disagree about when this point has been reached, so it's a decision you may need to work through yourself. It's true that some people just 'know' – it's a gut feeling and they are certain there's no turning back. Many others are far less certain about what to do and procrastinate endlessly or find it impossible to make a decision either way.

From years of listening to people's break-up stories I've pieced together some of the questions that I've asked that have seemed to help them resolve whether their relationship is over or there's something to revive.

Deciding whether to stay in or leave a relationship is a major life choice, and it deserves time, space and serious reflection. You can't do this kind of thinking properly while watching TV or squashed under someone's armpit on the train. Set aside a quiet moment when you're alone and undistracted. You're about to take an honest look at what you want from a relationship – and whether your current one has the potential to meet those needs, either now or in the future. It's not easy – very few people find this kind of self-reflection straightforward – but going through a few structured questions can help make things clearer. You might want to jot down your answers and revisit them later, especially when your mood or perspective has shifted.

Sometimes, distance helps bring the truth into focus. (And remember to keep your notes private.)

Set 1: Understanding your relationship

This first set of questions is about tuning into your current relationship dynamics and emotional reality.

1. Are your emotional, physical and practical needs being met in this relationship?
2. Do you have a clear sense of what your needs are, in the first place?
3. Do you believe your partner is capable of meeting – or willing to meet – those needs?
4. When you imagine your life without your partner, how do you feel? Relieved? Anxious? Sad? Free? Be honest.
5. When conflict arises, do you and your partner resolve it in a healthy, constructive way?
6. Have the issues that trouble you been part of the relationship for a long time, or are they more recent?
7. Are any of these 'red flag' behaviours present: constant criticism, contempt (e.g. name-calling), defensiveness (e.g. always blaming the other) or stonewalling (i.e. shutting down or withdrawing)? These are considered strong predictors of relationship breakdown.

Set 2: Exploring possibilities for change

This next set helps you assess what change might look like – and whether it feels realistic. You can work through these on your own or, if possible, with your partner.

1. List what's making you unhappy in the relationship. Be specific – try to avoid vague statements like 'we just don't connect anymore' and instead point to particular behaviours, patterns or unmet needs.
2. List what changes you're willing to make – and what changes you hope your partner would be willing to make. Again, be specific.
3. Do you believe meaningful change is possible? Is there genuine willingness and motivation on both sides to do the work required?
4. Based on your answers, how do you feel about the future of your relationship? Write a short reflection summing up your thoughts.

This process isn't about finding a clear yes or no right away – it's about gaining clarity. Whether you choose to leave, stay or seek outside support (like counselling), taking the time to think deeply and honestly is a powerful first step. Whatever decision you make, you deserve a relationship that feels safe, respectful and fulfilling.

Counselling

If you're still unsure about whether to stay or go, then speaking with a relationship counsellor can be very helpful. Counselling provides a neutral, calm environment where you can both feel comfortable to discuss any issues or problems openly. It's usually best for you both to go along and start the process of exploration together as it rarely works starting the process alone and inviting your partner to join later.

A counsellor should enable you to talk through your issues without being sidetracked and help you to manage your emotions when they are likely to be running high. While counselling might lead to reconciliation it can also lead to better communication and understanding between partners, giving more clarity on why a relationship has broken down, which can prove invaluable whether you stay together or decide to separate.

If you've committed time to working through your problems, have tried counselling but still decide to part ways, then you'll know that you arrived at that decision calmly and with consideration.

NOTE: if you know your relationship is over and a reconciliation will never happen, do not go along with counselling in the hope that it might salvage things. The anger and betrayal that your partner might feel is potentially huge and can have a derailing effect on the rest of the separation. If you go ahead with counselling, you could admit that you're not convinced it will salvage the relationship, but it could help for you to end it well, and it is certainly a worthwhile process for that reason. By doing this you've set your stall out and nobody is going with false hope.

> ### Case study: Joe and Kate
>
> *Joe, a former teacher, and Kate, a home educator, met at university and went on to have two children. Here they explain how, after counselling, they together accepted that their marriage had run its course and made a joint decision to end it amicably, agreeing that 'If we can't have the best marriage, we're going to have the best divorce.'*
>
> **Kate:** We had some relationship counselling at the start of 2020. We had tried to work things out but it was proving really hard so we got some professional help. That was really interesting and I found out some things about Joe that I'd never known despite the fact that we'd been a couple for around eighteen years. There's just something about the therapeutic environment that allows those things to come out.
>
> So the relationship counselling did help. It helped us to understand each other better but it didn't fix things.
>
> Then during the pandemic lockdown Joe was not needed at his school. So he was at home and, for a good

chunk of 2020, we had an excellent time. The children had both parents at home, we were having adventures, the weather was lovely. It was fantastic.

At the end of that summer, Joe had a family bereavement, which brought up a lot of grief. And then it became apparent that actually, when it gets really hard, we were not turning to each other for support. There were other people in our lives who provided better support.

And so, we asked a friend to look after the children, and we just went for a walk. And by the end of the walk, we said, shall we just split up? But we both said it, which was really nice because we both agreed that it was the right time. It wasn't one of us pushing and the other one resisting or anything like that.

I think we just drifted for a long time. And then eventually agreed, let's change things from here.

Joe: We always wanted to make sure that we tried to work things out, and I think the relationship counselling was an attempt to do that. But what we discovered was we were still friends, that we have this long history and there was still a lot of mutual admiration for some of our unique quirks. And while that period of time during the lockdown was really nice, we thought, well, we function quite well as a team, but not as a couple, and whatever was left of the couple wasn't really there anymore.

> It kind of got us back together so that we could then do this divorce well. It cleared the decks and got us to a place where we can work this out and do things as nicely as we can.

Separation

If you're questioning your relationship or deciding to end it, you might go through a period of separation first. A temporary separation can give you time to recover and reflect on your situation, while also giving you and your partner the comfort of knowing that the door of reconciliation is still open as you deliberate your next steps. At the same time, separation can also be profoundly disorientating, an ambiguous, muddled phase that can mess with your emotions.

Separation can of course take many forms and can occur before anyone has talked about a permanent break or in the period after you've made a joint decision to part. A small minority of couples might choose to legally separate – a process outlined on page 56 – but for most people separation is an informal agreement or arrangement between couples living apart. You might move out for a short while, staying with family or friends, or you might decide to move out permanently. Like many couples, you might continue to live under the same roof, to avoid the prohibitive cost of running two homes before any permanent or financial settlements have been agreed. If you have children, you might do the same in a bid to minimise disruption and to maintain a stable home life for as long as possible.

As a result, separation means different things to different people, and from a legal and emotional perspective it's ill-defined and there are no set rules to the form it takes. So woolly is the concept of separation, that often people are unsure whether they can define themselves as 'separated'. Can you put the term 'separated' on official forms? Do you have to declare yourself as 'separated'?

The answer is no: you can declare yourself as separated without involving legal systems or formal agreements, and this applies to marriages, civil partnerships and those in an unmarried relationship. (If you want, however, you can choose to formally separate, as outlined on page 56.) I can remember during my first divorce, when we had initially decided to live apart, being really worried about making it clear we had separated. It felt like a big, important change to me, but I didn't feel as though anybody else was particularly bothered, and I was surprised to learn that you don't have to report or record the fact!

In the early stages of a relationship breakdown or separation, you may not have told many people or even anyone what is happening. You might feel it's a private matter and you want to ensure things seem as normal as you can to the outside world, despite the tumult going on at home. You may have only just articulated to another person or your partner that the relationship is at an end; up until then your doubts and resolutions had just been in your head. As soon as you say it out loud you move into another phase of the emotional journey – and these are all important markers in the process of separation.

NOTE: if you have decided that your relationship is over and agreed to separate, I advise that you make a note of the date, and the easiest way of doing this is to send an email to each other. You could acknowledge the discussion you had, the conclusion you have reached, and that you agree you are now separated. That way you have a time stamp on the decision, which can have relevance further down the line when you're sorting out a separation or divorce formally.

Should I move out?

This is a question I am frequently asked. Lawyers often tell couples not to move out during a separation because in a contested case they might lose some leverage. For example, if a partner is in the house there is less incentive for them to make decisions quickly, or for the person who has moved out it might demonstrate they don't need the property or have a role to play with children.

My advice, however, is to do whatever is best for your children and for you. If you can, talk it through with your partner and try to figure out if you can realistically coexist in the same property. If one of you is able to move out, how would that work? Some relationship counsellors advise couples to physically separate if they can afford it as it can be challenging to live together under the same roof if you've decided the relationship is over, nor is it necessarily beneficial for children.

In short, you need to work out what is best for you and your family depending on finances, the dynamic between you and your partner, logistics with children and a host of other factors. If one of you does move out, you might consider the following:

- Which one of you will move out?
- Is it affordable to rent a short-term property and for how long?
- How will you work the logistics for children and spending time with them?
- How will you communicate when you need to?
- How will you care for any pets or deal with any house maintenance?

Nesting

One option that has gained in popularity as attitudes towards separation have changed is nesting. This is where children remain in the family home and each parent takes turns living there with them when it's their

> childcare days/week. That way the children get used to the idea you are separating but they are staying in the same home. It requires you to have somewhere to stay when it's not your parenting time – perhaps with a friend or relative if it's a short-term arrangement, or a rented flat or room if it's longer term.
>
> If you choose the nesting option, rotating in and out of the family home, you'll need to agree on issues like food, housework and laundry, and you'll be dealing with each other's paraphernalia around the home. It can work very effectively in the short term but it can be hard to maintain beyond that, unless you are able to operate comfortable separate spaces for each of you when out of the family home. When it works, it can be a great option.

Living together when separated

If, like many couples, you can't afford the luxury of nesting and you continue living in the same household when separated, it's important you establish some boundaries. Anyone who knows me knows how much I love a boundary in all aspects of my life – and at no point is it more important than when you are separating and living in close proximity.

If communication has broken down, setting boundaries can be difficult. Try to be clear to your partner about what works for you, and you may have to review everything as you go along. The kind of issues you need to consider will depend in part on whether you have told your children, if you have any – a key aspect of separation which is covered in Chapter 6. Here is what to consider:

- Where will each of you sleep – in a spare room, or will you need to convert an existing room into a bedroom, or sleep in your child's room? Or will you sleep in the same bed? (This might be the case if you haven't spoken to your children but it is very emotionally draining and not advisable if you can avoid it.)
- Will you still eat together?
- Will you buy separate food and cook separately?
- How will you divide household chores? This may have been a contentious issue for you in the past, so how realistic is it for you to figure this out reasonably?
- How will you do laundry?
- Do you need to agree over the use of cars or any devices in the house?
- Will the way you pay for things change? Are there new rules about spending from a joint account? Financial changes should always be discussed with your partner rather than making a unilateral decision.
- What are the rules around socialising and visitors coming to your home, or family members staying?

Separation agreement

While you're not required to formally declare a separation, you can draw up a formal agreement with your partner. This is known as a separation agreement (also called a deed of separation), and can be used to set out how you'll divide your money and property when you end your relationship and stop living together as a couple. A separation agreement is not automatically legally binding in the way a court order is, but if properly drafted – with both partners taking independent legal advice, providing full financial disclosure, and entering freely – courts will usually uphold it as evidence of your intentions.

You can have a separation agreement for ending a marriage, a civil partnership or a cohabiting relationship. The agreement sets out things like who will pay the rent or mortgage, which bills you will each pay, whether one person will pay any child or spousal maintenance and what will happen to the proceeds of sale if a property or asset is sold. A separation agreement can include intentions regarding pensions, but only a court order on divorce or dissolution (a pension sharing order) can legally divide a pension.

In cases where you have been married for less than a year or you have a strong religious objection to a divorce, you can consider a legal separation (sometimes called a judicial separation). A legal separation follows a similar process to submitting a divorce application (previously called the divorce petition) and requires a court fee to be paid, just like in a divorce. For most people, it is not necessary to legally separate – an informal separation will suffice until you choose to divorce. When should you have a separation agreement?

- **If you're not ready to divorce.** If you want to legally document your financial arrangements but are not ready to divorce, a separation agreement will enable you to divide your money and property without starting divorce proceedings. However, it's important to remember the agreement is not enforceable by the court – if you want a fully enforceable order you'll need to divorce and ask the court to make a financial or consent order (more on this to follow).
- **If there's a chance of reconciliation.** If you want some breathing space to decide whether you and your partner should divorce or end your civil partnership, a financial separation agreement allows you to outline how it could work without legalising things through the courts.
- **If your relationship ends when you're cohabiting.** A separation agreement will legally document how you and your partner should divide your money and property if you're not married and you separate. You and your partner can create a separation agreement, or you can use a company like *amicable*

or another legal professional to ensure it is properly drafted and legally valid.

A separation agreement can serve as a foundation for a future divorce settlement. It can then be turned into a financial consent order by the court if you go on to divorce.

When it comes to cohabiting couples, a separation agreement doesn't go through court and isn't automatically legally enforceable. It is a contract, and so it can be used as persuasive evidence in court if a claim between a separated couple arises at a later point. However, the court doesn't have the power to enforce it automatically. A court is unlikely to 'uphold' a separation agreement, if

- it's deemed unfair
- either person lacked access to legal advice
- there's been a material change in circumstances; or
- there's a lack of full and honest financial disclosure

'I want a divorce'

If you decide you want to end your marriage, you'll need to communicate this to your partner. This is a step so many people inadvertently forget about in the belief their partner knows, or that it's obvious, or they must have said it at some point in past discussions. When I ask people explicitly whether they have told their partner that the marriage is over and they want a divorce, you'd be surprised how many admit they haven't had this direct conversation. It's easy to believe that you are both on the same page because things have reached a point where you are barely talking. However, making assumptions is the undoing of many an amicable divorce, so this is an important step.

You might have been thinking about ending your relationship for a long time, but to articulate it and say it out loud marks a profound turning point. Despite the circumstances or atmosphere in the home, your decision may come as a huge shock to your spouse. You may have been unsure how your partner would react, which might have led to you putting it off or struggling with how best to broach the subject.

If you are at the point of no return but unsure what to say or how to approach your partner, here are some tips on how to keep the conversation as amicable and as calm as possible.

Step 1: Prepare yourself

Think about, or even write down, what you want to convey to your partner. The more shocked they are, the more volatile their reaction might be. Remember they are likely to be in a very different emotional place to you – see the diagram on page 38. The relationship may have been breaking down for some time but you will probably be further ahead in that emotional curve.

For that reason, be understanding – don't expect them to be okay or to agree with you straight away. You've had longer to process the situation than they have. You could rehearse what you're going to say with a divorce coach or counsellor or even the mirror, but the key is to know what you want to convey. Don't wing it.

Step 2: Pick your moment

Plan to tell your partner when you can be together one on one without interruption. Do not bring it up during an argument or in front of the children, other family or friends. If you can, do not have the conversation over the phone, be it an audio or video call or via text. Try to sit down in person, where you can see each other and therefore hopefully better understand each other's emotions. Going for a walk can also be a good idea as walking side by side, not having to make eye contact, can make for a less confrontational set-up.

Step 3: Keep the conversation short

Keep what you want to say simple and try not to stray into other, related, topics. It can be tempting – especially if you're in the 'explore' or 'commit' part of the emotional journey – to deliver the news that you want a divorce, but you've spoken to someone, they can sort it all out and there's nothing to worry about ... That's too much – you need to focus on the one important piece of news, along the lines of: 'I'm really sorry, I know this isn't necessarily what you want, but for me the relationship is over, and I don't want to continue with it.' You may have to repeat that, but keep it simple for now.

The natural response for someone at the receiving end of your decision is to react in an extreme way: 'You're not having the house!' or 'You'll never see the kids again!' They might be angry or even terrified of what happens next, and a conversation can rapidly escalate into a battle of words. Try not to react to any threats – appreciate that they have been dealt potentially the biggest blow of their lives and that attack is often the first line of defence.

If your partner tries to dig into the detail, you can respond with something along the lines of: 'We'll work that out, nothing will change immediately. We've got time to go through all of this properly but for now we need to focus on where we are emotionally.' Do not, in a bid to calm the situation, offer financial or practical solutions – focus on how you and your partner are feeling, let that be your priority and deal with the financial or legal implications further down the line.

Step 4: Be patient

Don't rush your partner. Learning that your other half wants to end the relationship can be devastating, like, as one person put it to me, putting all your personal belongings on a blanket and having them thrown in the air. Lives are turned upside down, and the shock can lead to intense feelings of betrayal, anger and fear, to the point of feeling numb and emotionally frozen.

Remember your partner has only just begun that emotional journey – their first reaction may be total disbelief or denial that anything was wrong, feelings that you may have had months or years before but have worked through. All of these feelings are valid and natural and your partner needs time to process these emotions. Rush them, or force them to move quickly and make decisions when they're not ready, and problems or unresolved emotional issues may bubble up further down the line.

If you are patient and set the right tone from the outset, it's more likely that relations and negotiations between you and your partner will remain amicable as you go through the process of divorce or separation.

How long is too long?

The most frequent question I am asked by an initiating partner is 'how long do I give my partner before they should be ready to negotiate?' It's natural to want to understand the timelines on an event like a divorce, but each case is individual and so many factors affect how people deal with this kind of news, so it's impossible to give one answer.

What I do know is that people often underestimate the time needed for someone to process the news that their partner wants a divorce or separation. It's not unreasonable to expect some kind of progress (just small steps, like making interim decisions) in three to six months, but I've had clients take much longer to work through things with their partners before they feel ready to move on to the next stage of divorce. Many an amicable divorce has been lost to impatience. The old adage is true, time is a great healer – so this is the time to channel your inner patience and give your partner space.

The emotional readiness of each partner in divorce or separation negotiations is perhaps the biggest predictor of whether you can achieve an amicable divorce, so getting the timing right is important (see page 98 for further information on emotional readiness).

If you feel your partner is 'stuck' and unable to accept the situation or move on, it might be beneficial to visit a counsellor or divorce specialist to talk through your options.

Case study: When are you ready?

Sometimes it can take a long time for couples to adjust to the fact that they are separating. To achieve an amicable divorce, however, both partners need to be ready to proceed. Being patient on this can prove really worthwhile.

A year ago, a client contacted me to say that he wanted to divorce his wife. They had been together for ten years, married for five, and had no children. Soon after they married, he realised it had been a mistake and had been unhappy since, although they still lived together in the same property. He told his wife of his decision to pursue a divorce but she did not take the news well. As a result, he felt that they both needed time to adjust to the situation and for his wife to understand the practicalities of life after the divorce.

He recently got back in touch to say that he and his wife were on good terms, in close contact and in full agreement on a practical and financial level. (The finances were a little unusual as he had inherited money quite young and his wife, who was from the US, had been concerned about visa issues after a divorce.) They now felt ready to proceed with the divorce and were keen to do so as amicably as possible.

When I asked him what had happened in the intervening year to get them to this place, he said: 'Well, at first we kept having the same "why" conversation. Why did I feel that way? Why was I leaving? Why didn't I love her anymore? She was really stuck in a kind of denial about the fact that I felt the way I did and to be honest I struggled to find the words to explain my feelings. I knew how I felt, but I'm not really used to talking about my feelings so I didn't have easy answers or anything that she could really hang on to.'

I asked him what changed, and he smiled wryly and said – time. He told me that once he let go of his own urgency to get things sorted, it gave his wife time to process her feelings, and, slowly, she started to engage in conversations that moved from why to what. What would happen to his wife's visa was much easier to answer than why he didn't love her. He could help her find out information that reassured her and meant she felt safe and ready to make some practical decisions about their future apart.

He told me that it wasn't easy, that they went back and forth and had a couple of big rows when he got ahead of himself and pushed too hard. But he knew that his wife would be capable of getting over it in the end – he just had to allow her to process it all in her own time. This way he was able to get what he wanted, which was an amicable divorce and a life apart.

The recipient

It may be that your partner has communicated to you they want a divorce or separation. Whether you had a feeling things weren't right or the news was entirely unexpected, you're likely to be in a very different place emotionally to your partner. Whereas they might have come to terms with the fact that your relationship was over, you might be feeling shocked, discombobulated or even devastated and in no way ready to move on (see the emotional journey diagram on page 38).

So, what can you do to help yourself as you get to grips with the news?

- **Don't isolate yourself.** It may help to talk to a trusted friend or family member who can offer support or listen to how you are feeling. They may not have all the answers – and it's probably best if they don't offer too many opinions right now – but listening and validating what you're going through can be a comfort. It's a fact of life that you need to teach people how to help you, so be clear with them: 'I just want you to listen', 'Please don't badmouth Charlie', etc. You might also consider talking to a therapist or other outside professional who could help untangle some of your feelings and perhaps offer a different perspective to the thoughts spinning around in your head.
- **Prepare for grief.** Divorce can induce such feelings – you're losing someone you thought you'd share your life with – but unlike death, that person continues to exist and you may well need to continue to interact with them, particularly if you have children. This complicates the grieving process so it's not surprising if you experience seesawing emotions, one moment acute sadness and the next relief. It can induce an identity crisis – who am I if I'm not married? – knocking your self-esteem and sense of self. You might experience sleep problems, appetite changes and other physical symptoms, just as you might if you were going through a bereavement.

- **Know when to get help and when to self-soothe.**
  If you feel very low, anxious or depressed, visit your GP, try counselling or get help from a therapist. It's important to look after yourself from the outset – do positive things for your body, rather than self-medicating with alcohol, food or staying out late. The key is to do these things in moderation and not let it become something you rely on to get you through the emotional side of divorce. In the early days, focus on the basics of life and don't pressure yourself to do too much.
- **Try to maintain familiar routines that will give you some sense of normality**. It's easy to underestimate how much eating regular meals, getting rest and some fresh air on a walk can help support your body and mind. Daylight (particularly in the early morning) and walking are my go-to antidotes to low mood.
- **Give yourself permission to feel.** It's completely normal to experience a mix of conflicting emotions at first and you need to give yourself permission to feel these. Doing this without judgement can ease the emotional load you're feeling. Journalling and writing down your thoughts, however raw or unfiltered, can be a powerful way to clear your mind and gain some perspective on how you're feeling.
- **Remind yourself about the emotional journey of separation** (see the diagram on page 38). Right now, you may be experiencing turbulent feelings and you

may question whether the relationship is really over, but over time you will move towards acceptance. If your partner has instigated the separation, they will be further along the emotional journey. For now, you need time to absorb the news before engaging in discussion with your partner, who has likely had more time to consider their options and may already feel ready to discuss practicalities.

- **Ask for time.** If you don't feel ready to have further discussion, then voice this firmly and kindly. If you feel able, reassure your partner that you want to do things amicably, but you'll feel better equipped to do so if you have some time to process things. How much time you'll need will of course vary from person to person and according to your circumstances, but, if it helps to have an estimate of time, three months is reasonable. By doing so, you've given yourself just a little control over the situation at a time when you might be feeling adrift.
- **Stop reacting, start responding.** If on receiving the news you reacted in a strong way, perhaps with shouting or tears, which was understandable at the time but it's not how you usually behave, just draw a line under that. You can always explain to your partner that your behaviour was a response to shocking news (and perhaps entirely deserved!) but that's not how you want to go forward from here.

Case study: The three G's

Hearing the news that a partner has decided to end a relationship, and it's clear that no amount of conversation will change their mind, is not only a huge shock but can also leave many people with lots of unanswered questions. Broadcaster Paul Roseby, whom I interviewed for a podcast, explained how painful it was to receive the news out of the blue and how he coped in the aftermath.

Paul and his husband had met over twenty years ago and they went on to have a loving, happy relationship. Paul described his divorce journey as being made up of three G's: Grief, for the emotion you feel when divorcing; Grit, the resilience to get you through the day; and Gratitude, acknowledging the love and happiness you had.

The day it happened we were in Portugal where I had met a celebrant not long before as I was thinking about renewing our vows! I really thought we were good. And then that evening, I was told that we weren't. And that was it. It really was. There was no debate … It was just: 'I don't want to be married to you after all.'

Flying back to the UK, all I could think about was, okay, I need to save our marriage and do what I can do to fix things. But his reaction was that it was over. There was no conversation after that at all. There was no hope within the marriage – it was done. I suggested we go to therapy, but he said he wasn't going to change his mind.

I went into absolute panic mode ... I wasn't angry, but desperately upset, desperately hurt. It was like an inner scream and giving voice to that would have diminished its power. The pain was that strong.

My instinct was to survive and not dive into it emotionally with him. We continued living in the same house together for a while, which I thought was the only option because I didn't want my world to completely crumble. But I felt that I was living on borrowed time and that the world we had built together was going to be taken away from me. I was trying to work out what the hell I was going to do. I look back and think what a shame we didn't talk more. We were both in shock. He threw the punch and I tried to avoid it.

It was a really humbling experience – we were living a brilliant life, a dream, and then that dream was broken. I tried to go back to the person I was before I met him, but rejection really eats into your identity and sense of self, and sometimes it's just enough to get through the day.

Once I'd moved out, I did therapy to try and find my balance living with grief, disappointment and rejection. I'm in a much better place but I still wonder if I could have done things differently.

When I was going through it all, I developed coping mechanisms, things I could control, and even the smallest things can make all the difference. I would make the bed in the morning. I would exercise. I would say yes to being invited out even though I didn't really want to go out. Bit by bit that builds your confidence and you start to regain your independence.

If you're living with somebody who doesn't want to live with you anymore, if you can find it in your power to be kind, despite everything, it will absolutely build you, give you a sense of achievement, when you leave. Remember who you are and remember why somebody wanted to be with you in the first place. And you're still that person.

And absolutely, there is happiness and joy around the corner. It might just be quite a big corner. Honestly, just be kind to yourself and love yourself.

And don't forget to breathe.

In summary

- Accepting the reality that a relationship is at an end can be tough, and deciding whether to stay or leave deserves time, space and serious reflection.
- Articulating to your partner that you want to end your relationship marks a profound turning point. It's likely that you and your partner will be at very different places emotionally.
- If you are the instigator don't rush your partner as they will need to process what can be devastating news. If you are patient, it's more likely you and your partner will remain amicable.

- If you choose to separate but still live together, you need to create boundaries.
- Hearing that your partner wants a divorce can be devastating and disorientating, but it is the start of a new chapter, not the end of your story. Divorce is a unique kind of loss, but like any grieving process, the pain does soften with time, support and self-compassion.

3

The Choice Is (Y)ours

Whether you instigated the end of your relationship, or the decision was made for you, at some point you'll need to explore what happens next. You may not feel ready, and you may resent being rushed, or having to instigate the next steps, but at the end of the day 'doing nothing' is not a long-term option and you will have to engage eventually.

You'll need to start thinking about the practicalities and how you legally end your marriage or partnership. Exploring and gaining an understanding of the options can help you set off amicably and prepare you for the journey ahead even if you're not emotionally ready to take formal steps. And if the timing is out of your hands, it will help you to feel more in control. Let's go over the basics – the process and terminology – when it comes to divorce and separation.

If you're married, the legal process to end your marriage is divorce; if you're in a civil partnership, it's dissolution – but the legal steps for both are the same. In the past, the first step in getting a divorce was to instruct a solicitor, but times have changed, as has the law, and there are now many other ways to legally end a marriage or civil partnership that are kinder, less expensive and less likely to lead to escalation. In sorting your finances there are some processes that allow you to be more collaborative and amicable than others and you'll need to decide which work best for you and will help you get to where you need to be.

It's important to clear up some terminology here. Legally speaking, a 'divorce' is simply the unpicking of the legal marriage and nothing more. But when we commonly talk about getting divorced, we are also referring to arrangements concerning money and property (known as the 'financial remedy' process), and those concerning children.

Arrangements for children are ideally dealt with in a parenting plan. We have the 'no order principle' in England and Wales which means an order should only be made if it's in the best interests of the child – so parents are encouraged to stay out of the courts on matters concerning children unless there are safeguarding issues or an intractable dispute. Financial matters are best agreed in a consent order. A really important point here is that simply divorcing does not end your financial relationship with your partner and this can mean they can claim against your assets in the future – particularly worrying if you think you might build up a pension or inherit money.

Online you might find divorce companies offering to help with the legal paperwork for a surprisingly low fee, but this alone doesn't sort out all aspects of a separation and it's often the negotiations over the finances and children that take more time to navigate successfully.

At one end of the scale, you can go through the courts and a judge will make a decision for you on issues that you cannot agree on with your partner. At the other end, you can go through a very informal process – a DIY or kitchen-table agreement – where you settle everything yourself and you have a very casual, loose arrangement. Between those two poles there are various other processes that will help you to come up with a legally binding agreement, which ideally you want to have so you are protected both now and in the future.

If relations between you and your partner have broken down entirely – in that you cannot be in the same room together – then you may need to go through a solicitor and eventually the court. But if you can communicate with your partner, even if only in a minimal way, then you may well be able to choose a more amicable option, which could cost you significantly less money and result in a far more positive outcome, especially if you are going on to co-parent children after separation.

Understanding the three aspects of a divorce will help you to choose a service that works for you and your partner.

1. Legal unpicking of the marriage

The divorce process involves the following steps:

- Divorce application made
- Acknowledgement sent from the court
- Divorce issued by the court
- Twenty-week reflection completed
- Application for a conditional order
- Consent order submitted
- Consent order approved
- Application and granting of final order

The official process involves submitting a divorce application. You can do this yourself on the gov.uk website or you can ask someone to do it for you, such as a solicitor or divorce specialist. It's not a difficult process, rather an administrative one. The fee at the time of writing is £612 (see page 130 for more information on fees and exemptions).

There then follows a twenty-week 'cooling-off period', built in to ensure that if your partner hasn't given any warning of their intent to divorce, you have some time at least to get your head around it. If you're on board with the divorce or have been thinking about it for a while, twenty weeks can feel like a long time to wait, although many people start collecting their financial information together or making parenting arrangements during this period. After twenty weeks, you then apply for a conditional divorce (formerly known as a decree nisi), and the court gives permission for the divorce. It's important to note that having permission and being divorced are not the same thing!

Once you have permission to divorce, you can apply for a consent order (not mandatory but in my view a must-do) which covers agreements relating to finances and ends the possibility of claims in the future. Then six weeks and one day later you can apply for the final order (formerly the decree absolute). Assuming the application is deemed fair and legally sound, the court then legally dissolves the marriage.

The divorce process takes a minimum of thirty-five weeks, and if you are applying for a consent order (and I cannot say this enough times – I recommend you do so!) then the process takes about ten months.

When you apply you need only state that your marriage has irretrievably broken down (you don't need to say why) and you can choose either a sole application as an individual, where you divorce your partner, or a joint application where you divorce each other. About 75 per cent of divorces in England and Wales are made by sole applicants, whereas at *amicable* about 75 per cent of cases are joint applications. (See page 130 for more information about the difference between these applications and how to choose what's right for you.)

2. Arrangements concerning children

When it comes to children, unless there are safeguarding issues or intractable disputes, arrangements should be sorted out privately by parents and shouldn't be matters for the court or court orders. Sadly, the judiciary doesn't enforce this with any rigour and lots of solicitors encourage parents to obtain child arrangements orders by consent – something I strongly feel is unnecessary and throws parents into the pathway of the court if the orders are not followed to the letter.

You will need to agree on where your children live, when they see both of you, who will pay for what and how you will raise them – this is called a **parenting plan** (see page 171). By doing this first you ensure your financial decisions fit with what is best for your children and that any money to do with them (i.e. child maintenance) is covered by the financial remedy process.

3. Money and property (the 'financial remedy' process)

You need to agree on what will happen to your home, where you will live in the future and also what money, debts and assets you have to divide (a 'financial disclosure' – Chapter 8). To make your agreement legally binding you will need to submit a consent order with your divorce paperwork. This usually includes a clean break order which protects you against any future financial claims, which again I strongly advise you have, even if you don't have any financial assets to split (see page 141 for further information).

The different processes for divorce and separation

There are various ways to sort out money and property when you end a relationship. Here are the main options ranging from more informal methods, which involve minimal input from legal professionals and where you make your own decisions, to full-blown court hearings where a judge will decide for you.

Do-it-yourself

A do-it-yourself or 'kitchen-table' agreement involves couples negotiating the terms of their financial settlement themselves with minimal input from legal professionals. This includes agreeing arrangements for children and the division of money, property and pensions. It's the most cost-effective option but carries risks and requires time, effort and the emotional headspace to understand the legal process and where to find accurate information.

For this or any kind of settlement to be legally binding it must be written into a consent order, as mentioned above, accompanied by a full and frank financial disclosure.

Key features: Couples need to be able to communicate well and agree on most aspects of their separation, including all the financials. This is the most cost-effective way to divorce.

Pitfalls: There is the potential of making a mistake and one person might dominate the negotiation leading to an unfair outcome. Negotiating a divorce can be emotionally challenging and having a neutral third party like a divorce specialist or mediator can be helpful. Also, you don't know what you don't know – it's easy to miss something or to believe that equal and fair mean the same thing – in divorce they don't!

Mediation

A mediator is an independent, trained professional who helps you and your partner to work out agreements for children (parenting plan) and finances (consent order). It's a more amicable alternative to lengthy and expensive solicitor negotiations or court proceedings.

Key features: You need only one mediator (unlike solicitors where you need one each), making it a less expensive option. It also saves time – government figures show that via mediation it takes couples on average four months to resolve their issues, whereas via other processes, such as using solicitors, it takes on average thirteen months.

Pitfalls: Your partner may not agree to mediation or you might fail to make progress with the process. A legal professional or divorce specialist is still needed to turn what you have agreed into a consent order and this can often raise issues with the agreement, adding extra costs or risking the agreement being unpicked. If you can't agree then you may still end up going through the courts.

Negotiation services such as *amicable*

Companies like *amicable* provide a more comprehensive service than mediation, giving help with negotiation and communication, as well as the entire legal process. We can also help you reach agreement on financial and childcare arrangements. It means you can separate without lawyers and our fixed fees make it more affordable.

Key features: Factoring in the emotional journey of divorce, our divorce specialists guide you through negotiations and parenting plans, and explore multiple options for pensions, property and finances. Our consent order specialist can draft your consent order and liaise with the court on your behalf. *amicable* helps couples reach a fair and reasonable agreement that prioritises the whole family (particularly any children) rather than just one individual.

Pitfalls: More expensive than the DIY option, although we have fixed fees and payment plans that allow you to spread the cost over several months for no additional cost. If relations between you and your partner have broken down entirely or are abusive or coercive then we won't be the right service for you. If you can't agree then you may still end up going through the courts.

Consent order write-up services

amicable and other companies also provide a less expensive consent order drafting service. If you have reached an agreement through mediation, kitchen-table or solicitor negotiations, our service can write up the consent order and send it to the court.

Key features: You can do an online disclosure including telling us about your agreement. We will draft your consent order and send it to the court for you, taking care of all court correspondence. This means you will have a legally binding agreement and potentially a clean break, protecting you from future claims. We have arrangements with lots of mediators – so if mediation is your preferred route, check to see if your mediator will send your agreement to us to write up.

Pitfalls: More expensive than the DIY option. You need to both agree this is the right way forward, and as with all consent orders you must both do a full, frank, transparent disclosure.

> ### Case study: Four happy parents
> *When embarking on the divorce journey it is a good idea to think about what you want the future to look like. What kind of relationship do you want with your ex and how can you achieve that? When I start working with couples, we discuss what their goals are for the future and encourage them to remind themselves of this as they go through the process. Here one of our divorce specialists, who is also a*

> *former divorce lawyer, explains how this is one of the key differences in the amicable process.*

We start off with a goals session. I've been so impressed and delighted by people volunteering what they want – for example, they want to be at their children's graduations or weddings together. Having been a divorce lawyer in practice for over twenty years, I found this a complete revelation because it's the opposite of how a lot of people would approach the divorce process with their respective lawyers.

It resonates for me because my parents divorced in the 1980s. It must have been amicable, because I knew very little of the process and we always came together for birthdays and family events. They eventually had new partners and I always used to say as a kid that I had four happy parents, not two unhappy parents. If you can manage that, it really makes a difference for children, and you take that into your life.

Solicitors

This is the most commonly used divorce option and is suitable for couples who want to avoid contact with each other or where the protection of the law is required (a partner is hiding or disposing of assets, for example). Each person has a solicitor, which makes this the more expensive option.

A solicitor can manage the entire legal process and deal with your partner's solicitor and the court, and can make protective applications to the court where required. A more cooperative way of using solicitors is through the collaborative law process where solicitors sit down together and work with the couple alongside financial and co-parenting experts to sort things out as a team.

Key features: A solicitor will try to get the best deal for you as an individual and they will ensure everything is legally binding. They'll manage the whole process and advise that you don't have any direct contact with your partner.

Pitfalls: Tends to be more of an adversarial, confrontational process as the lawyer works for you as an individual rather than the family, which can have an impact on co-parenting and future relations. Lawyers tend to charge on an hourly basis and costs can mount up quickly, especially if negotiations are protracted. Collaborative law tends to be very expensive but avoids some of the pitfalls of a traditional lawyerly approach.

> ### Case study: Grin and bear it
> *The common assumption is that a divorce will be a long-drawn-out legal battle and a serious drain on finances. For that reason, couples often stay in an unhappy relationship for far too long and for all the wrong reasons. One of our divorce specialists worked with a couple who fell into that*

category and were sadly unaware how relatively straightforward a divorce could be.

I worked with a couple who admitted that their relationship had been over for a very long time but neither of them had had the courage to divorce. They'd had a son together and because they thought a divorce would just be too hard on all of them, they thought they would just grin and bear it until the son was older.

The husband said to me afterwards that had he known how straightforward it was going to be they would have done it years ago. Choosing the *amicable* process was the best decision they made, and a real lifesaver, although it is sad to think all the anguish they experienced over the years could have been avoided.

Going to court

The majority of divorces do not require a court appearance. However, sometimes negotiations break down and you need a judge to decide for you in court. This can be one of the most acrimonious and expensive paths to take for divorce, although it's rarely the choice of both partners and sometimes it is the only way forward.

Key features: Situations that can result in ending up in the courts include: your partner refuses to negotiate or go to mediation; you are in an abusive or violent relationship and it is not safe to negotiate; your partner is not giving full disclosure of assets; you're not making any progress in mediation or with solicitors.

Pitfalls: Costs of hiring a solicitor and a barrister if your case goes to a final hearing are high. Figures suggest that the average cost of a divorce going through court is £40,000 per person in London, and £13,000 per person outside of London. Resolving matters through the courts also takes longer, potentially twelve to eighteen months.

Arbitration

Instead of a judge in a court making decisions on issues that you haven't been able to agree on, you can appoint an arbitrator to do this. They can make decisions about all or part of your finances and children's arrangements that will be final and binding.

Key features: Arbitration hearings are private and this is especially important as the court transparency project ramps up and judges are encouraged to publish judgments and allow press reporting in court rooms. They are generally quicker than going through court and a good option if you have reached a sticking point that cannot be resolved as part of negotiation, mediation or solicitor-led services.

Pitfalls: Arbitration is voluntary so if one spouse refuses to take part the process won't work. Certain cases, particularly concerning child protection or safeguarding, cannot be arbitrated. Hourly rates can be high.

A final word on the *amicable* approach

When I made the sad decision that my second marriage was over, I was terrified about how my ex-partner and I were going to sort stuff out. I knew we'd have to talk about the kids and where we could both live and who would get what in terms of savings, pensions and financial support.

So, like a lot of people, I thought that mediation would be the best way forward. What scared me, however, was how I was going to hold my own in mediation with a man who negotiated for a living.

I understand now, having talked to thousands of divorcing couples through my work at *amicable*, that this is a common fear. Mediation works well when the playing field is level and the agreement you're coming to fits squarely in the middle of what the courts find acceptable. But there are some downsides to mediation, and this is made evident by the falling numbers of people using it to sort out their finances in a divorce.

We set up *amicable* to bring together the best bits of mediation but also add a level of intervention and advice that mediation often lacks. Our divorce specialists are legally trained, but more importantly they are empath specialists skilled in conflict management and navigating the emotional journey of divorce. They are trained in what the law says, but also can be partisan where needed and offer negotiation support to help you apply the law to your circumstances. They don't take sides, but neither will we leave it up to you to navigate unchartered territory – and that's why 95 per cent of couples who use the *amicable* service end up with an agreement ratified by the court.

In summary

- The divorce process itself is now simpler and less adversarial than it used to be, and involves an application, a twenty-week reflection period, a conditional order, and finally the legal dissolution. It takes a minimum of thirty-five weeks to complete, and if you are having a consent order this extends to around ten months, sometimes longer depending on the speed of your financial negotiations.
- Alongside the legal process, couples must decide how to handle property, money and children's needs. A 'divorce' is simply the unpicking of the legal marriage – arrangements for the care of children and sorting out finances are different processes.
- To make a financial agreement legally binding, you need to submit a consent order – also called a financial order – with your divorce paperwork.

- Options range from DIY or kitchen-table agreements to mediation, specialist negotiation services like *amicable*, or solicitor involvement.
- The common assumption is that divorce will be a long-drawn-out legal battle. It doesn't have to be and can be relatively straightforward and amicable if couples are able to work together.

4

What Is an Amicable Divorce?

We hear it all the time: 'I just want an amicable divorce.' The word 'amicable' tends to mean the best you can get when it comes to separating or divorcing. And in March 2014, actor Gwyneth Paltrow and musician Chris Martin cemented it as an aspiration when they announced they were splitting up via a technique called 'conscious uncoupling'.

A year later, they finalised their divorce, having remained on amicable terms and co-parented successfully, demonstrating publicly to the world that it could be done. Love them or loathe them, they were trailblazers for amicable divorces everywhere. And while some might say it's easier to be amicable when you're super-rich, the change in the narrative was palpable. More than a decade on, the idea of an amicable divorce is not so rare (thank you, Gwyneth and Chris) and it is my mission to make it the norm.

Unlike the traditional legal route for divorce, which sets partners on opposing sides and discourages direct communication, the *amicable* process helps couples to work together and actively encourages open dialogue. This can of course be challenging, and for some couples it's a big ask, but it's so inspiring how many get through the process and reach an agreement that works best for their needs and circumstances. In doing so, they retain a good working relationship with one another, which has a huge benefit for future family life.

There are three core components of an amicable divorce: **communication, cooperation** and **mutual respect**, techniques for which are outlined in this chapter. The process won't tell you *why* your relationship has broken down – a counsellor or therapist can help you to explore that – but it will enable you to work through all the financial and legal tasks of a divorce and separation. In doing so, you may need to set aside any past or current grievances so you can focus on the practicalities, but you may also find some issues naturally resolve themselves along the way or that you come out of the process in a better place than where you began.

If you're aspiring to have an amicable divorce then you'll get the most benefit if you avoid the traditional solicitor route and try to work with your partner rather than against them. And yet if you are having to go through solicitors – even if you're being dragged through the courts by your partner – being mindful of what makes an amicable divorce and employing some of these techniques could help to diffuse further conflict.

You might think that an amicable divorce is an unrealistic prospect for you and your partner. Perhaps communication is very limited and there's still a lot of hurt and resentment between you. With some patience and careful guidance, however, I have seen many couples, where perhaps one partner is still deeply upset, manage to get through the process. They have been able to control their emotions, deal with the tasks at hand, and even grow in strength as they do so. After all, what is the alternative? Engage lawyers, cut off all direct communication between you and your partner, and battle it out? How does that improve the situation?

There are of course circumstances where an amicable divorce won't be possible: if there is abusive or coercive behaviour in your relationship then you may need the protection of a lawyer, or if one partner refuses to cooperate in any way or communication is entirely unrealistic. It is, however, a good objective for many types of couples, from those who are still co-operative and respectful of each other, to those who need more support to communicate or who are in very different places emotionally (see the diagram on page 38). As couples are more in control of the process, they can move at their own pace, pause for further discussion or guidance, and still reach their intended goal. I have helped many couples navigate the difficult emotional journey, some of whom had little confidence they could see it through, and achieve an amicable separation and a positive new start in life.

Emotional readiness

Wherever you are on the journey, to achieve an amicable divorce or separation, you and your partner need to be in agreement that your relationship is at an end and that you now need to separate formally. This doesn't mean that both of you necessarily *want* the relationship to end – it's more the acknowledgement that if one of you wants to end the relationship, it is over. You need to feel able to work with your partner and to make decisions that are beneficial for both of you. You may still be feeling sad or a range of negative emotions, but can you control these feelings, think rationally and make decisions about your future? Are you and your partner emotionally ready to begin the process of an amicable divorce or separation?

To check for emotional readiness, you should ask yourself some questions. These include whether you feel blame or anger towards your partner for the split and whether you have a sense of hope for the future, questions that are often dictated by who instigated the divorce and when you first learned of the end of the relationship. The questions are designed to dig a little deeper into the circumstances of the break-up and to see whether an amicable separation is a realistic option at this stage. It may be that you haven't yet processed the idea of a divorce – you might still be in the denial, anger or resistance phase, which are all perfectly natural feelings, but you may need a little more time before you engage in the process.

Some of the questions also shed more light on the current dynamic between you and your partner, and it's worth considering them as you embark on the process. You may not 'like' your partner right now, but can you still attribute some positive qualities to them? Can you remember what you liked about them when you met? Perhaps they cheated on you but can you hold on to the concept that they might be a good parent? Can you interact with your partner, despite how you might feel about them, in a polite and calm way?

Here are examples of signs of what we term low, medium and high emotional readiness, which may help you decide if you're ready to move ahead with an amicable divorce or separation.

Signs of low emotional readiness

~ You have yet to come to terms with the break-up, are feeling raw and unable to control your emotions (such as shock, anger and denial).
~ You are thinking about your own pain and focusing mainly on what went wrong with the relationship.
~ You feel guilty or you want to blame your partner for the situation you're in.

All of these reactions are perfectly normal. It can take several weeks or even months to process a break-up, longer if it's more of a shock or your partner initiated the break-up. If it's been three to six months since one of you ended the relationship, you could consider some professional emotional support like a counsellor, divorce coach or therapist to help you process these emotions – see the Resources section for further information. If you are feeling this way and your partner starts the divorce, you will be legally required to respond so think about how you can get a team of support around you to help you cope.

Signs of medium emotional readiness

- You have good days and bad days. You have come to terms with some aspects of the end of the relationship, but you still have lingering unhelpful emotions that make talking to your partner difficult.
- You can probably start conversations with your partner and make some progress, although certain issues trigger arguments and it's difficult to get your point across.
- You feel ready for a working relationship with your partner but you are not sure you can trust them to do the right thing.
- You or your partner say you are ready but in practice there are still signs of resistance.

An amicable divorce or separation may be more of an aspiration right now, but with a little support or time you could be ready. Divorce or separation specialists can oversee and set boundaries in conversations, and help you manage the emotional journey as well as the legal and financial aspects of a separation. Take a look also at the essential elements that make up an amicable divorce and see if you can work on these so you can achieve a working relationship.

Signs of high emotional readiness

- You accept you've reached the end of your relationship, even if it wasn't your choice, and are ready to explore what the future holds.
- You may still have your off-days but you can manage your emotions and are able to express your needs in a calm way.
- You are focused on what's best in the long term for your children, if you have any.
- You are both keen to move ahead and negotiate a fair agreement.

You are ready to move ahead with an *amicable* divorce or separation, working with a divorce or separation specialist or via an automated *amicable* service.

> ## Case study: Keeping dialogue open
> *When I begin working with couples, they are sometimes in very different places emotionally and communication can*

> be challenging. However, we deliberately encourage them to communicate, keeping them in that hot space that can be uncomfortable, but which facilitates open dialogue and encourages resolution rather than division. Sometimes we even see a transformation during the process – people can grow in confidence, which helps them to find happiness after the separation.
>
> Here, one of our divorce specialists talks about a couple she recently worked with.

Paul and Kay had three young children, and he worked while she didn't. Paul had had an affair and when I first met Kay she was distressed and at a very low ebb, saying things like 'I'm never going to be anything. I'm useless.' She would often get upset talking to me and during sessions, which Paul found difficult.

Despite this, we managed to work through the process, step by step, which, in a way, acted as a comfort blanket for Kay. Knowing that she would have regular meetings with a clear agenda and structure and that she could ask questions and debrief afterwards helped Kay to organise her thinking and process the tasks that needed to be done. This meant that Paul could see that constructive progress was being made even though he wanted to go faster at first. The structure allowed him to be patient. And so, we got to a final agreement. With my help Kay was able to control her emotions, and this meant there was space for discussions not just to get an agreement but to check it worked for them both. It also meant they could make better decisions about the kids, knowing the finances were sorted.

What particularly struck me, however, was how well Kay was after the whole process. She had changed from being a tearful, unsure and 'deserted' (as she put it) woman to a very confident person who had begun work and now had a great job. Two years later, I did an introductory session with her and Paul and his new partner to facilitate blended family living and she was like a different person. Kay and Paul both said they were so pleased that they'd done it this way. Kay was just really happy; she had met someone else, and they were able to work as a blended amicable family with their new partners.

Kay said that being able to speak to Paul during the process really helped. She could ask questions and he apologised for a couple of things along the way. He was also able to acknowledge what happened and accept how hard things had been, which can only happen if you keep that dialogue open. We are not a therapy service, but we give couples a chance to raise things they may not have raised before, talk about them and move on.

As mentioned above, the key elements of an amicable divorce or separation are communication, cooperation and respect. I don't expect the process to be entirely smooth –

there will be disagreement – but there are methods you can learn to manage potential conflict and to keep dialogue open, respectful and constructive. Remember, relations with your partner need not be perfect but just 'good enough' so you both feel able to express your views and make rational decisions about finances and the future.

Communication

Effective communication is key to an amicable divorce. This can be a challenge as communication breakdown is the key driver for divorce and separation – 44 per cent of respondents in a Danish study of 2019 cited communication problems as a major contributory factor behind their separation. If you're both at the stage of accepting your relationship is at an end and have a common goal, then effective communication is made easier and can be a positive outcome of an amicable divorce.

The traditional legal route of divorce discourages direct communication between partners, deepening division and adding confusion along the way. Typically, lawyers send out letters, often cloaked in complex legalese, which the recipient receives without any warning. (There's nothing like receiving a legal letter to get the adrenaline pumping out of sheer fear of what it might contain.) The recipient, now on red alert, may misconstrue the meaning of the letter – or the lawyer writing it may have misinterpreted their client's instruction in the first place – leading to significant delays or endless back and forth. Lawyers may then proceed to argue over points that were never an issue with the clients, all the while billing for the extra time involved and ratcheting up the conflict and stress levels for everyone involved.

During my second divorce, I certainly found it difficult to behave in an amicable way when I was being provoked at every turn. After a while I fell into the trap of anticipating or expecting a hostile response, and I began to read hostility into everything. It's a race to the bottom when you're both experiencing your separation in those terms, and it doesn't usually end well.

Mixed messages

The divorce or separation process, particularly when it comes to financial or legal details, can easily lead to miscommunication or errors in understanding. For example, in England and Wales the starting point for a divorce is based on an equal division of assets, a 50/50 split. That split, however, can be adjusted in line with various factors and circumstances, one of which is 'need'. If one person has greater need than the other – perhaps because they are to be the main carer for the children and have lower earning capability – the split may have to be adjusted in their favour.

> Two lawyers could explain this to their respective clients, but if you're the partner with the higher income, you might zone in on the 50/50 division and assume there will be an equal split. If you're the other partner, you might focus on the 'need' element and assume you will receive more than half because you have greater need. The information becomes distorted, perhaps because the lawyers didn't check that their clients understood the nuance of the issue. As the couple are no longer communicating, and only liaise with their individual lawyer, they haven't heard each other's perspective or understanding.
>
> If they were working together as a couple, with someone explaining the issue to both of them at the same time, then any misunderstandings could be cleared up there and then, nipping any confusion or disagreement in the bud before it became a problem. Disputes over the division of assets are one of the most commons reasons couples end up in court and are the source of so many entrenched arguments during separation.

Effective communication allows issues to be discussed, clarified and resolved by each partner. Here's how you can maintain effective communication during the separation or divorce process.

1. Express your needs and concerns clearly. Try not to be vague or expect the other person to work out what you want. Sometimes people can't pinpoint why they feel uneasy or that something is wrong, or they find it difficult to articulate how they feel. You might need another person, like a divorce specialist, to help unpick what is causing any unease, which might then help you to express yourself or understand the consequences of a certain issue.

2. When communicating, make sure you have been understood and don't just assume so. You could do this by asking what the other person thinks. It might become evident that they're unclear about what's been communicated or feel uncomfortable about certain issues. At that point you can go over things and unpick some of the detail, and clear up any confusion or disagreement before it snowballs into a major issue.

    In working with couples, I might ask each partner to play back or summarise what someone has just said, just to encourage open dialogue and to make sure everyone has digested all the detail. Disagreements often stem from people not understanding what's being asked of them, so keeping those communication channels open is incredibly beneficial.

3. It also helps if you have a clear sense of what you want before entering into any dialogue. To do this, set aside

time so that you have the headspace to think things through properly. We lead busy lives and are all so distracted that you may need to block out time to think about what your needs are, both now and in the future.

Key areas to consider are: where you will live, whether you will have enough money to live on day to day, and what your plan is for retirement. The court, who approve your agreement, can't magic up pensions and property if you don't have them – its main job is to make sure that one of you is not left in a worse situation than the other because of the role you played in the marriage.

The wider world

At some point you'll need to inform your family, friends, workplace and the wider world in general about your divorce or separation. It's an issue that can cause some anxiety and needs careful thought and planning. Top of these concerns is how to tell your children, and we'll cover this in more detail in Chapter 6.

It's best if you agree with your partner when you will tell people and what the key message will be. It really is unsettling if one of you bumps into someone who seemingly knows everything about what you thought was a private matter between you and your partner. Conversely, you shouldn't feel that you can't speak to anyone during the process, as emotional support is important at this time.

what is an amicable divorce?

When you and your partner decide to let a few more people know about your situation, it's best to agree on what you're going to say and to whom. It really is up to you how you do this, but here is a sample communication plan that some couples I work with use for some ideas.

Recipient	Key message	Delivery mechanism	Timing
Children	We love you very much. We're not together as a couple anymore, but we're still your parents and always will be.	Face-to-face, age-appropriate conversation	Before any wider announcements
Close family	We've decided to separate but are doing so amicably and with mutual respect. Please support us both equally.	Phone call or in-person chat	Shortly after telling children
Close friends	We're separating but it's been thoughtful and respectful. We'd appreciate kindness and there's no need to take sides.	Phone call or message, followed by conversation if needed	Shortly after family is told
School / childcare	We're no longer together but are co-parenting positively. Please communicate with both of us equally about the children.	Email or in person, depending on usual communication	As soon as practical after the decision is final

amicable divorce

Recipient	Key message	Delivery mechanism	Timing
Colleagues	Just letting you know we're separating. It's amicable, and we're still working together respectfully.	Direct message or short conversation	As needed, ideally after friends/family have been informed
Social media / Wider circle	We're separating but are grateful for our time together. We're focused on positive co-parenting. Please don't speculate or speak negatively.	Email, online message or social media post if appropriate	Once key people have been informed directly

My advice generally when working with couples is that less is more when it comes to telling friends and wider family. If you purposely haven't told your children or close family members, the more people you tell, the more likely they will find out. Some couples find it easier to post something on social media or email their news, which means they don't have to tell people individually, but if you choose that option think carefully about the wording and make sure you both agree to it and you are clear on whether settings are private or anyone can see the message.

Again, the wording you opt for is entirely your choice, but here's a sample social media post written by a couple with children who are intending to divorce and co-parent amicably.

We have some personal news to share.

After a lot of thought, love and care, we've decided to end our relationship as a couple. It's a sad moment, but also one filled with gratitude for the years we've shared, the memories we've made, and – most of all – the amazing children we've brought into the world together.

We're still a family, just in a different shape now. Our focus is on being the best co-parents we can be, with kindness, respect and a shared commitment to our children's happiness and security.

We know people may have questions, but we're not going to talk about the ins and outs of why or how we got here. What matters is where we go next, and we're doing that as a united parenting team.

Please don't take sides or speak negatively about either of us. We're proud of how we're handling this, and your support means the world when it's rooted in positivity and love for all of us.

Thank you 💜

If you talk to friends or family, as is entirely natural, you need to make sure that they don't influence you too much. If your friends, in the belief they're being supportive, badmouth your partner or share their own 'battle stories', your goal of an amicable divorce, which involves you making decisions with your partner and possibly co-parenting with them in the future, will become more of a challenge.

Yes, your partner may be insufferable or have cheated on you, but it doesn't help if people around you inflame any hurt or anger you're feeling. To avoid this, have a pre-conversation with your friends – preferably before you've opened a bottle of wine – along the lines of: 'Look, I may complain about Alex but just hear me out, you don't have to agree or join in.' It's a little like if you were complaining about a close member of your family – a brother or your mother, perhaps – your friends might feel it wasn't their place to join in. It's a similar situation with your partner. Explain that you're trying to keep things amicable, you want to avoid conflict and scarring legal battles, and this is your primary goal for now. You may need to vent and let off some steam, but it's enough if they just listen and provide a shoulder for support.

Cooperation

Cooperation is a way of managing any conflict and finding common ground so you can reach a mutually beneficial agreement. You may disagree and not get on with your partner but it's helpful if you can recognise they have a right to feel certain things and have some good qualities. This comes with acknowledgement that you once had a loving relationship and shared a life together.

Communication between partners can easily escalate into conflict, particularly if feelings of anger, hurt or betrayal are at play. Dialogue can ramp up into a fierce argument, as emotions take over and people start firing barbs at each other rather than communicating in an effective way. This is natural and common among couples, but it's useful to take a step back and look at the dynamics behind conflict of this kind.

A typical scenario involves one person saying something, perhaps a relatively minor criticism, which triggers an extreme reaction from the other person because they feel threatened. They misjudge the situation as dangerous, as an imagined threat, and consequently respond in an aggressively defensive way.

The other person then feels personally attacked and might try to defend themselves or respond to what they perceive is an overblown reaction. Even if they try to calmly explain things, they are still exacerbating the situation and the conflict cycle continues. They might be tempted to apologise but this will only reinforce the idea that that person has done something wrong.

Respect and the EAR technique

There are ways to break the conflict cycle, to calm and neutralise the situation before tempers are raised even further. Your partner's response is not so much about the issue at stake, it's more about feelings of being attacked and their mistaken perception of threat, so this needs to be addressed. The best way to do this is to employ the

EAR (empathy, attention, respect) technique, as devised by conflict specialist and therapist Bill Eddy.

E – Empathy
Show you understand how they feel, even if you don't agree with why they feel that way.
> *'I can hear that this is really worrying for you.'*
> *'It sounds like this has been frustrating.'*

A – Attention
Give them your full focus. You don't have to agree with the issue, but showing that you're listening matters.
> *'I understand that this is important to you.'*
> *'I want to make sure I'm hearing your concern.'*

R – Respect
Acknowledge the concern without dismissing it.
> *'I'll listen while you explain what's going on.'*
> *'Your perspective matters to me; tell me more.'*

Perhaps the simplest technique to employ is to state your intention for cooperation up front. Remind yourselves of the future relationship you want – whether co-parenting smoothly or maintaining respect – before sending any message.

At times you may well disagree with your partner but this doesn't mean you have to get angry or upset. If you feel tensions rising, remember you don't have to respond immediately – you can take a pause, rethink and come back to your partner when both of you have calmed down. Try not to ratchet things up to prove a point – if you're aiming for an amicable split, you need to try to put unhelpful feelings to one side and to focus on the tasks at hand.

Conversely, don't nod along to everything because you're frightened of conflict. Try to speak up or take time to talk to a divorce specialist or a therapist, as you need to be able to express what you want or talk through issues. The last thing you want is, two years after your separation, to think to yourself, why on earth did I agree to that!

ABC of separation (the *amicable* behaviour charter)

Maintaining effective communication, cooperation and respect during a divorce or separation eases the whole process, and this feeds into your behaviour. Couples who achieve an amicable divorce behave in a certain way, as is evident with the many couples I work with at *amicable*. Note, these are normal couples, with different personality types, financial or family backgrounds; they are not 'saints' with superhuman levels of self-control. What sets them apart is their behaviour, which helps them to communicate effectively with their partner and work through the various tasks.

As you move through the divorce or separation, focus on the future rather than getting stuck in a discussion about why your relationship has broken down. While that's a valid process, it's not the objective of an amicable divorce, which is to end the relationship and deal with the financial, legal and parenting issues involved. (Coming to terms with the emotional breakdown of the relationship is more of a therapeutic, healing journey, which can run alongside the practical journey.)

The following table shows the type of behaviour you should aim for and what you should avoid. I ask couples to commit to a version of this at the outset of their divorce journey with us and it's useful to refer to it as you go through the process and after the divorce if you're co-parenting or still in touch. Think of it as a practical checklist to make sure you're in the right space.

What to aim for	What to avoid
A focus on the future and the interests of children, if you have any	Dwelling on the past, focusing on individual rights or legal claims
Integrity and trust – a future co-parenting relationship is built on trust	Putting the other person down or badmouthing them
Honesty – being open and honest with the information you provide, even if it seems contrary to your interests to do so	Hiding or distorting information when asked for it
Respect and kindness	Being critical, using sarcasm or speaking for the other person

What to aim for	What to avoid
Patience and an ability to see the other person's concerns and perspective, even if it means the process moves slower	Interrupting (don't worry, you will get a chance to be heard)
A focus on the underlying things that are important to you, such as a future co-parenting relationship	Making threats or issuing ultimatums
A creative and constructive approach to problem-solving	Becoming fixed to one point or strategy and criticising when someone changes their mind
A commitment to moving the process forward and trying to meet deadlines	Not speaking up or expressing your point of view if something doesn't work for you

Here are some more tips on behaviour, communication techniques and managing potential conflict:

1. *Regulate before you communicate*
   Take a breath, pause, or even step away before responding to something emotional. Ask yourself: 'Will this comment help or harm the tone of this conversation?' Use grounding techniques like repeating a calming phrase (e.g. 'stay focused, stay kind').

2. *Keep a calm tone and body language*
   Speak slowly, use a soft and steady tone, and avoid pointing or pacing. Keep your hands open and at your sides (closed posture or crossed arms signal defensiveness).

3. *Use 'I' statements instead of 'you' accusations*
   'I feel anxious when I don't know the plan for the weekend', rather than 'You never tell me what's going on!' This reduces blame and invites dialogue rather than defence. When referring to your partner with another person use first names rather than 'he' or 'she'.

4. *Actively listen without interruption*
   Reflect back on what you heard: 'So what I'm hearing is that you want to keep the handover time consistent?' Validation doesn't mean agreement – it just means acknowledging their point of view.

5. *Stay solution-focused, not blame-focused*
   Ask: 'What can we do next?' rather than 'Why did this happen?'

   If things feel stuck, try a 'yes, and ...' instead of 'no, but ...'

6. *Stick to one issue at a time*
   Don't bring in history or multiple topics. Focus on one clear point. If things go off-track, gently say: 'Let's come back to this later. Can we finish this one first?'

7. *Pause digital messages when emotions are high*
   Don't fire off texts or emails when upset – wait twenty-four hours if possible. Avoid getting into online messaging or email arguments. Reread messages before

sending them and ask yourself: 'Would I be okay if someone read this out in court or in front of our kids?'

8. *Take responsibility for your part*
Even if the other person is upset, take ownership if you were misunderstood. 'I can see how what I said came across badly. That wasn't my intention.'

9. *Set time limits and breaks for big conversations*
Agree in advance to keep conversations short (no more than 30 minutes). Build in the right to pause if either of you becomes overwhelmed. Set parameters and agree to talk or have meetings only during business hours (9 a.m. – 5 p.m.) or at a fixed time outside work. This can also apply to emails and messages.

10. *Remind yourselves: it's about moving forward, not winning*
Keep a shared phrase in mind like 'What matters most is remaining good co-parents.'

Resistance

In working with couples, I sometimes see more subtle signs of resistance as we work through the various tasks and discussions. It may be that one person isn't engaging fully with the process or they say they are ready but they are doing things to stall: perhaps they say they haven't got time to look at certain documents or are nitpicking.

This kind of resistance can cause problems later in the process so it's a good idea to address it when you see it and resolve any concerns early on. Here are the kinds of techniques some of our divorce specialists employ and which might prove useful to you when liaising with your partner.

Spot the signs of resistance early

Clues are:
- Repeated delays reviewing or signing paperwork
- Overfocus on small details or disagreements
- Avoidance/rescheduling of meetings or key decisions
- Contradictory behaviour (saying 'I'm fine with it', but acting contrarily)

To deal with this you might say: 'I'm noticing we've come back to this a few times and it's not moving forward – do you think there's something else going on underneath?'

Use reflective, non-judgemental language

Rather than confronting resistance, explore it: 'It's really common to hit a point like this' or 'It sounds like part of you wants to get this done, and another part is hesitant. Can we talk about both sides of that?' The aim is not to force action, but to help the person own their ambivalence.

Uncover underlying fears or beliefs

Resistance is rarely about the thing being resisted. It's often a cover for fear of change or the unknown, or an expression of guilt, shame, regret or reaching that final emotional hurdle (e.g. 'Signing this means it's really over').

Shift from pressure to empowerment

If someone isn't ready, pressure often backfires. As a result, reframe questions in a bid to lower defensiveness and encourage ownership of the situation. 'What pace feels sustainable for you right now?' instead of 'You have to get this done'; and 'What would need to happen for this to feel more manageable?' instead of 'Why haven't you done this yet?'

Collaborate on a plan to move forward

Once resistance is acknowledged, you can then rework things practically:

- Adjust timelines without stalling indefinitely
- Break tasks into smaller chunks
- Agree on new check-in points

For example: 'How about you just look over Section 1 today, and we'll revisit the rest next week?'

amicable divorce

If you're trying to work with your partner at home to move your separation forward, here are some more phrases that might help:

- 'I wonder if this might be more emotionally loaded than it looks?'
- 'What feels hardest about this part for you?'
- 'Would it help to pause and look at this again next week, or does it feel better to tackle it now and get it off our plate?'
- 'Is there a small, manageable issue we can agree on today?'

Dos and don'ts checklist for an amicable divorce

DOs – Behaviours that support an amicable divorce	DON'Ts – Behaviours that undermine amicability
Keep communication calm, short and respectful, as if you're writing to a work colleague.	Don't use blame or guilt. 'This is your fault' or 'You're abandoning us' only hardens positions.
Focus on the future, not the past. Think about what you both need moving forward.	Don't bring up old arguments as it derails forward progress.
Use 'I' statements – 'I feel ...' vs. 'You never ...'.	Don't involve the children in adult matters, even subtly.
Acknowledge emotions without being ruled by them. 'This is hard, and I still want us to work through it well.'	Don't make assumptions about motives. Ask, don't guess.

Give space when needed, especially if one person is processing the situation more slowly.	Don't use legal threats casually. This will create fear and escalate tension.
Prioritise the children's well-being above everything, even if your relationship is strained.	Don't use social media to vent or share private details. You will regret it and it may ruin your reputation and credibility.
Stick to facts, agreements and deadlines. Be reliable and consistent.	Don't insist on being 'right'. Focus on fair, not perfect.
Be honest and clear about your needs. Don't be evasive or ambiguous about what you want.	Don't talk negatively about your partner to mutual friends or family. Doing so spreads toxicity.
Raise concerns early and constructively before resentment builds.	Don't rush the other person if they're processing things more slowly as this can create resistance.
Ask for help from a coach, mediator or therapist when things feel stuck.	Don't expect to agree on everything. Aim for 'good enough' solutions.

In summary

- Amicable means working *with*, not *against*, each other, focusing on communication, cooperation and respect to create a fair and peaceful separation that supports everyone involved.
- Emotional readiness is essential, as being able to manage feelings and think clearly allows both partners to make calm, practical decisions about the future.

- Clear, honest communication transforms the process, helping couples avoid misunderstandings, reduce conflict and stay focused on solutions rather than blame.
- Cooperation and respect build stability, and using empathy, patience and kindness makes it easier to listen, compromise and keep discussions productive.
- Behaviour shapes outcomes, so staying calm, honest and future-focused leads to fairer agreements and healthier post-divorce relationships.

5

D-I-V-O-R-C-E

So sang Tammy Wynette ... and if ever a subject was made for country and western music, with all the lament associated with the end of a relationship, it is divorce. The love that once burned brightly has dimmed, as have the shared dreams of a life together, and letting go of all of that can drag you through every emotion possible – even if you know in your bones it's the right decision for you and your future.

While the personal journey of divorce and separation can feel intense, thankfully the legal process of ending a marriage has become a little more straightforward and, importantly, kinder. Since 6 April 2022, you no longer need to give a reason why your marriage or civil partnership has broken down; you or your partner need simply to state that it has and that's enough for the court to proceed with the process. This change in the divorce laws applies to England and Wales. (Scotland and Northern Ireland are separate jurisdictions and have different rules – see the Resources section for further information.)

Prior to the change in the divorce laws, many couples who had thought long and hard about whether to divorce, concluding perhaps that the relationship had simply run its course, were shocked to discover that unless they had been separated for two years, one of them needed to accuse the other of being at fault. That system, thankfully, is no more – couples no longer need to play the blame game in a process that now focuses more on resolution than accusation, the fundamental basis of an amicable divorce.

While I certainly breathed a huge sigh of relief when the law changed, people sometimes still ask me whether they can use the older, fault-based system, perhaps because they want it formally recognised that their partner cheated on them or had caused the breakdown of the marriage. That isn't possible now – all new divorces and dissolutions must follow the Divorce, Dissolution and Separation Act, the key steps for which are outlined below. If you want that kind of validation – which, by the way, is perfectly natural – it's best to talk it through with a counsellor, therapist or trusted friend. The only exception is if your divorce application was submitted prior to 6 April 2022 and is still ongoing, in which case the previous system will still apply.

This chapter provides some detail on how to apply for a divorce or dissolution, and the legal and administrative tasks you need to complete to formally end your marriage or civil partnership.

To begin the process, you need to fill out a divorce application (previously called filing a petition), which can be found online at **gov.uk/divorce/file-for-divorce**, or, **gov.uk/end-civil-partnership/apply** for a civil partnership. These are fairly simple forms, and either you can fill them out yourself or a service provider can do them for you. There are a couple of sections that sometimes cause confusion, so I'll provide a little more information on these below. Here's what you will need:

- Your marriage or civil partnership certificate. You can order a copy on the government website. If you got married abroad you'll need to ensure your marriage is legally recognised in England and Wales and get a certified translation of your marriage certificate if it is not written in English. You can contact the foreign embassy or government of the country where you married for more information or to assist with this (and see below regarding further information on marriage outside of the UK).
- You will also need to provide your and your partner's name, home address and email address, and if your name is different to that on your marriage certificate you'll need to explain why or provide deed poll documentation. The court will send the divorce papers to you online but if you do not give an email address the papers will be sent by post.

~ There is, at the time of writing, a fee of £612 to submit an application. It's the same fee if you're making a sole or joint application – see below – and you might qualify for help with the fee if you are on a low income or benefits. Check **gov.uk/divorce** for further details on this.

Sole or joint application?

Early on in the application you must confirm whether you're making

- ~ a sole application – you or your partner are divorcing the other partner; or
- ~ a joint application – you are divorcing each other.

A sole application involves one spouse (the 'applicant') submitting the application, which the court checks and then sends to the other spouse (the 'respondent') with an 'acknowledgement of service' notification. The respondent is sent a notice of proceedings via post and/or email and instructions on how to complete the acknowledgement of service via the online portal.

In a joint application, both spouses submit the application as Applicants 1 and 2 and there is no separate sending of papers and no respondent. Once the case is issued by the court you will both be sent a link to confirm receipt of the issued application (or a letter if an email address wasn't supplied). In both cases the earliest you can apply for a divorce or dissolution is one year from the date of your marriage or civil partnership.

If only one of you wants to divorce, the other spouse cannot contest the application for any reason other than: (a) your marriage is not legally recognised in England and Wales; (b) you're already divorced; or (c) an English and Welsh court does not have the jurisdiction (legal authority) to deal with the divorce (see page 134).

If you submit a joint application and it stalls, perhaps because your spouse fails to take the necessary action to progress the application or there's a breakdown of communication, you can switch the application from joint to sole. It's not possible, however, to change a sole application to a joint application.

Prior to the reform of the divorce laws in 2022, only sole applications could be made, so the option to apply jointly is relatively new. According to gov.uk's family court statistics around 75 per cent of divorce applications in 2024 were made by sole applicants and 25 per cent by joint applicants – in part because of lack of awareness of the new joint option. With the couples I work with, it's the other way round – roughly 75 per cent make joint applications, principally because they have already agreed to work together, and this is something I strongly advise if you want an amicable divorce.

If you and your partner submit a joint application, the idea is you are divorcing each other, rather than one of you divorcing the other, and it gives you mutual control. Note that you don't have to be physically together to submit a joint application: you simply fill out the relevant sections in the application, which will be sent to your partner, and you can check each other's answers. Direct contact is not necessary at this stage.

Some people worry that a joint application means that both partners are equally to blame for the breakdown of the marriage. It doesn't – remember, we've moved away from the fault-based divorce system – and whether you make a joint or sole application bears no relation to how or why your marriage ended. In fact, the opposite is true: making a joint application can give you back control, particularly if you weren't the instigator of the break-up and feel swept up in the whole process. You can see and agree to every stage, make shared decisions and shape how the relationship ends even if the split wasn't your decision in the first place. It gives you a shared voice, some influence over timing and pace, and makes for better relations and peace of mind after the divorce has gone through.

The benefits of a joint divorce application:

- Encourages cooperation and mutual decision-making
- Gives both partners equal visibility and input at each stage
- Leads to fewer misunderstandings and less miscommunication

- Reduces potential for disputes and legal intervention
- Is generally more cost-effective if conflict is avoided
- Sets a healthy foundation for future co-parenting

However, a sole application may be needed if:

- Either of you feels strongly that they don't want to be the instigator in the divorce
- Your partner refuses to cooperate
- There has been domestic abuse or coercion in the relationship
- You intend to do a 'help with fees application' to negate or reduce the court fee and only one of you is on a low income

The application

Once you've chosen whether you are making a sole or joint application, you then move through the different sections of the form.

- Statement of irretrievable breakdown – simply tick 'yes' (and no fact or reason is needed)
- Applicants' details – full names, address(es) and contact details of Applicants 1 and 2
- Marriage – date, place, certificate details, proof of name change if applicable

- Fees – confirm whether you need help with fees
- Jurisdiction – confirm whether you and your partner's lives are mainly based in, or connected to, England and Wales
- Financial order – tick if you intend to apply for financial arrangements or child arrangements
- Upload your documents – take a photo or scan and upload documents, such as marriage certificate
- Statement of truth – you confirm all the information is accurate
- Pay the fee and submit

Jurisdiction

You'll be asked on what basis the court of England and Wales has jurisdiction (the legal authority) to deal with your application. Questions will include: *Is your life mainly based in England and Wales?* It goes on to say: 'this may include working, owning property, having children in school, or your main family life taking place in England or Wales'. If you or your partner mark 'yes' then you can apply for a divorce in England and Wales because you are habitually resident in England and Wales.

Jurisdiction is determined by the factors below, not by your nationality or where the marriage took place.

- Habitual residence: this is the place in which your life is mainly based. You must be settled there and intend to stay settled there. Some of the following may apply: you work there, own property, have your children in school there, and your main family life takes place there.
- Domicile: the place of your permanent home in which you live, or to which you intend to return. When you were born you will have acquired your parents' domicile (for example, your father's if they were married, or your mother's if they weren't married or if your father died before you were born). If you have since moved to another country and made that your permanent home then your domicile may have moved there.
- If you were born in England or Wales, lived your entire life here, and intend to stay here, then it is very likely that you'll be both habitually resident and domiciled here.

Note that more than one country can have jurisdiction at the same time. Just because you start divorce proceedings in another country doesn't mean you can't do the same in England and Wales providing these courts also have jurisdiction. You can find more information on this on the government website.

Recognition of divorce abroad

A common query I have from applicants is whether their divorce will be legally recognised overseas. Almost all countries will accept a divorce issued in England and Wales. However, as all documents are now processed online, some countries will query the lack of wet seal (a paper document that has been physically stamped or embossed with an official seal). The advice around this is confusing, not least because the providers that gov.uk suggests in order to get your documents 'legalised' won't accept the digital copies of your divorce that the court sends to you (because they don't have a wet seal!). You will need to ask the court to send you documents that have a wet seal.

If you need a wet seal, or for countries that will only accept a wet seal as proof of your divorce, you can send a completed D 180 form to the divorce court along with a copy of your final order (and a separate form for the sealed consent order if applicable) to request that the court provide a copy of the document with a wet seal. The court usually takes around two months to process this.

Some countries, such as Islamic states in the Middle East or other parts of Asia, may not recognise foreign divorces unless granted under their own religious or legal systems. If in doubt, check with the relevant country's embassy, to ascertain what documents are required as proof you are divorced.

Financial order

The divorce application also includes a question about whether you want to apply for a 'financial order', and for whom, with the following options to tick:

- myself
- the children
- no, I do not want to apply for a financial order

My advice? Tick 'myself', and if you have children, tick 'the children' also. Here's why.

What is a financial order?

A financial order is a legal document from the court that formalises the financial arrangements between you and your spouse. It outlines how you will separate any assets, debts, pensions and income once you're divorced or your civil partnership has been dissolved. A financial order is called a 'consent order' or 'financial order by consent' if you agree it with your partner rather than going to court and asking a judge to make a decision for you. The terms 'financial order' and 'consent order' are often used interchangeably on websites, and in this book we generally use the terms 'consent order' or 'financial order by consent' as our aim is that partners will agree on their financial arrangements.

Many people think that getting divorced ends the financial relationship with their partner, but a divorce only ends the marriage, allowing you to remarry again; it doesn't sever financial ties. If you don't add a legally binding financial order or consent order to your divorce, then you could be vulnerable to claims in the future.

If you can't agree on how to divide money and property, the court can make an order dictating how this should be done. This is called 'contested proceedings' and usually follows a series of financial hearings heard by a judge in court. It's a long and very expensive process – but if your spouse won't cooperate it's a necessary one. The cost for applying for this is currently £313 and you'll need to fill out a separate Form A – see gov.uk for details. Before applying, you also need to show the court that you've had a screening session with a mediator to see if your case is suitable for sorting things out together or that it's not safe for you to do so. This means sending the court a Mediation Information and Assessment Meeting (MIAM) certificate obtained from a mediation service, stating that you have tried and been unable to come to an agreement. You don't have to have had any joint sessions to get a MIAM certificate; it could simply be that your partner has been invited to attend and has said they don't want to engage, or it has come to light during one partner's initial sole meeting with the mediator that there is domestic violence.

A better alternative (if possible) is for you and your partner to come to an agreement yourselves, 'by consent'.

Perhaps you agree to split your savings, pensions and sell the house, but to make this legally binding your agreement must be documented formally as part of a financial consent order. You can get divorced without a financial order; it's not mandatory, but your ex could claim a share of your future wealth or assets (so long as *they* haven't remarried – even if you have), as the much-publicised case study on page 143 illustrates.

When applying for a financial order by consent, you are asking the court to approve the agreement you have made with your partner on how to divide your money and property after separation (see Chapter 8 for more information on how to do this). Note that the court is not deciding or making that agreement for you – as some people mistakenly believe – it's simply reviewing what you have agreed and deciding whether it's fair and fits within the bounds of English and Welsh law. The court can only accept or reject the order if you are doing it 'by consent' – they cannot make changes. The court might come back to you with queries if something appears to be missing, or request clarification if the agreement appears one-sided or doesn't account for certain assets (like pensions). The key here is that the court will only approve a financial order by consent if it seems fair and they are satisfied no one is being coerced.

A note of caution here: a judge doesn't know you or your family or your history, and they only have a very short amount of time to look over your paperwork, so agreeing to a settlement in the hope a judge will step in and reject it is risky and dangerous. By signing the consent order and submitting it to the court you are saying you are happy it's fair and you understand its implications.

There is an extra fee to apply for a consent order, currently £60, and a legal professional can help you prepare the consent order so that it is drafted correctly, is legally binding and gives you the protection you need. While you don't need a solicitor to draft up your consent order, you do need someone who understands the legal process and has experience in drafting a consent order.

So, to reiterate, when you are filling out the divorce application and confirming you want to apply for a financial order, tick 'myself'. You might think that's unnecessary if you have no assets or property to divide, but a financial order can also include 'clean break clauses' (see below) which protect you from future claims. Even if you decide that you only require child maintenance after separation, you should still tick both 'the children' and 'myself'.

Once you've ticked the boxes, you don't have to progress with the financial order – the court doesn't chase you for it. But if you don't tick the boxes and you later decide that you want to formally sort your finances out with your ex, then you'll be very limited over what type of order the court can make if you have already remarried. Your ex-partner might not have the same restrictions, as long as they have not remarried. It really is better to be safe than sorry!

Note that ticking the boxes doesn't protect you – you still have to make a separate application for a financial order. It's also worth noting that if you are remarrying, if you make the financial application to the court before you do so then the court can still make financial orders even if you remarry while the proceedings are 'live' or haven't reached their conclusion.

Formalising your financial arrangements requires full disclosure of all your assets and debts – see Chapter 8 for further information on this. Note that the court can't make your consent order legally binding until you've started your divorce and it has received your 'conditional order'. You can apply for a financial order at any time, even after the divorce is finalised. There is no strict time limit on this unless you remarry, after which you lose the right to make certain financial claims against your ex-partner. Be warned, however. If your ex dies *after* a final order of divorce but *before* a financial consent order is in place, the surviving ex-partner could lose any inheritance or financial provision that they would have otherwise received. It is therefore safer to get the consent order sealed by the court before finalising your divorce.

Clean break order

A consent order outlines the financial arrangements between you and your partner and will usually include a clean break order, dismissing any future claims against each other. Informally, there are two types of consent order:

1. A full consent order tells the court what 'financial transactions' will happen following your divorce, such as the sale of your home, sharing your pension or spousal maintenance, which usually contains a clean break clause.
2. A clean break consent order is used when there are no financial transactions taking place and records that you will each keep what you own, and there is no ability to make a claim against each other in the future.

You may not have any assets or finances to divide with your partner, but a clean break order will make sure that your ex can't make claims against you in the future. Without a clean break order your ex could make a claim on any income, bonuses or post-divorce assets such as future pensions, windfalls, inheritances, your business taking off or even lottery winnings (rare but possible!).

A full consent order may include a deferred clean break, such as a Mesher order. In this situation, a clean break may activate after a certain event, such as postponing the sale of the family home until your children have completed school or university (see page 238 for further information). A clean break on income may only be possible once child maintenance payments have stopped.

NOTE: The divorce application does not ask for information about your children (such as their names, ages, living arrangements or support). The court expects parents to make their own arrangements concerning children – see page 161 for more information on setting up a parenting plan. If you apply for a financial order, the D81 (a form that accompanies your consent order – see page 229) asks for the children's names, dates of birth, any agreed child maintenance payments and where they will live. You can also include child-related financial arrangements such as child maintenance or school fees orders in a financial consent order.

Case study: Dale Vince and Kathleen Wyatt

A widely publicised case involving green energy tycoon Dale Vince and his ex-wife Kathleen Wyatt serves as a cautionary tale for couples who neglect to settle financial issues during their divorce proceedings. Just as a financial order can be implemented at any point, even years after a divorce, so can a claim be made by either partner, in this case some thirty years after they separated.

Kathleen Wyatt and Dale Vince were a free-spirited couple who met in 1981 when Kathleen was 21 and had a young daughter, and Dale was 19. They married later that year, had a son together in 1983 and split up not long after. After the break-up Dale began travelling, initially converting an old ambulance into a camper van, and he went on to live on the road in various vehicles.

Kathleen raised their son, had two more children from a subsequent relationship, worked a variety of

amicable divorce

jobs but lived largely on benefits. In 1992 Kathleen divorced Dale and because they had little or no assets at the time of separation no financial order was made as part of the divorce.

Fast-forward a few years and Dale had gone from living in a van to building turbines and experimenting with wind power, before founding Ecotricity, one of Britain's leading green energy suppliers. He became a multi-millionaire and was awarded an OBE in 2004 for services to the environment and to the electricity industry.

In 2011, almost twenty years after their divorce, Kathleen issued an application for a financial settlement and a £1.9 million payout. As a financial order had not been made in the divorce, and she had not remarried since her divorce, she was entitled to make a claim, although the initial claim was rejected. The court did say she might have more success with a more modest claim, which would enable her to buy a home mortgage free.

As a result, in 2016 Kathleen was awarded a lump-sum payment of £300,000. The settlement was approved in the High Court by family judge Mr Justice Cobb, who said: 'I am perfectly satisfied that is reasonable, and that the wife is entitled to receive a modest capital award following the breakdown of the marriage.'

The moral of the story? Even if you have no money or assets to split, get yourself a clean break order.

Divorce timeline

So, what are the steps involved in getting a divorce? Let's go through the usual timeline:

Step 1 – Apply for the divorce

Submit either a joint or sole application for divorce. The court will check this and if satisfied with the information provided will issue your divorce application (usually within one to two weeks, but it can take as long as three to four weeks in busy periods).

If a sole application is sent, a copy is sent to the other spouse (the respondent) via email or by post if the applicant hasn't supplied an email address. The respondent must acknowledge receipt within fourteen days either via an online portal or, if no email address is provided, the court will send additional papers for the respondent to complete their acknowledgement. If the respondent doesn't acknowledge receipt you can apply for a deemed or dispensed service – see gov.uk.

Step 2 – The twenty-week 'cooling-off period'

Once the court issues your divorce application, you must wait for the twenty-week reflection period to elapse before progressing further. This is designed to give couples time to adjust to the news and make any financial arrangements or provisions for childcare.

Step 3 – Apply for the conditional order (previously called the decree nisi)

After twenty weeks you can apply for the conditional order, which is the middle stage of the divorce process.

Step 4 – The conditional order is granted

The court reviews your application and, if satisfied that you can divorce in England and Wales and all the information you have provided is correct, it will provide your 'certificate of entitlement' (to a divorce). This states the date your conditional order will be pronounced at court – though neither you nor your partner are expected to attend the court hearing. Once a judge has pronounced your conditional order, a six-week waiting period starts on the same day before you can apply for the final order.

Step 5 – Apply for a consent order (not mandatory, but advised)

As soon as you have received your conditional order certificate, you will be able to apply for a consent order. In order to legalise your financial split and end the possibility of claims in the future you can submit a financial consent order to the court and have this approved by a judge.

Step 6 – Apply for the final order (previously called the decree absolute)

Once the six-week period has elapsed after the conditional order is granted, you can apply for your final order. This is the final stage of the process. Once granted (this takes one to two days), you will receive a final order certificate which confirms that your divorce has been finalised and you are free to remarry if you wish. It's important to note that even if the six weeks' timeline has elapsed, you shouldn't apply for the final order until your financial order by consent has been approved. In addition, if you have a pension sharing order as part of your settlement (see page 148), you should wait twenty-eight days from the date on the consent order before applying for the final order.

Why do you have to wait for the final divorce order if there's a pension sharing order?

A pension sharing order forms part of a consent order and sets out how a pension will be divided. It only becomes effective on the *later* of:

- the date your final divorce order is granted; or
- twenty-eight days after the pension sharing order was approved by the court.

Until then, it cannot be enforced.

If you apply for your final divorce order straight away, the court may grant it before the twenty-eight days are up. If your ex-spouse dies in that gap, the order won't take effect – and because you'd already be divorced, you could lose any widow/widower pension benefits. By waiting twenty-eight days after the pension sharing order is approved before finalising your divorce, you stay protected. If your ex-spouse were to die during that time, you'd usually still be entitled to spousal death benefits. Once the twenty-eight days have passed, the pension sharing order will take effect and secure your pension rights. Although the extra wait might feel frustrating, it can be vital to protect your pension.

d-i-v-o-r-c-e

Cooling-off period

The twenty-week cooling-off period, which was introduced as part of the new divorce laws in 2022, is designed to allow couples to reflect and consider their situation and possibly reconcile if they want to. Where that's not possible it provides time for couples to agree important arrangements for the future, particularly concerning children and finances.

For some couples, such as those who have been separated for a long time or who have come to their decision after careful deliberation, twenty weeks can feel like an exceptionally long wait. There aren't any precise statistics on how many couples reconcile during the twenty-week period but it was suggested during parliamentary debates in 2020 that 5 to 10 per cent of divorces might be averted if couples were able to pause proceedings. The twenty weeks can only be reduced in exceptional circumstances, such as if one partner has a terminal illness, and this is decided by the court on a case-by-case basis.

There are of course plenty of things you can do during the twenty-week period, alongside reflecting on your decision to end your marriage. It's a good time to discuss and agree with your partner on any arrangements concerning children and to fill in a parenting plan. You can also locate financial documents – which can be a time-consuming process – and discuss financial matters to see if agreements can be reached. The subsequent chapters cover these crucial areas in more detail, helping you to reach a divorce agreement that works for you and family.

In summary

- No-fault divorce has simplified the law – now you need only confirm that the marriage has irretrievably broken down.
- You can choose a sole or joint application. A joint application encourages cooperation, gives both partners equal visibility, and reduces disputes. A sole application may be necessary if there's abuse or a lack of cooperation.
- A divorce does not end financial ties. Without a financial order (or clean break order), ex-partners can make claims on each other's assets or income years later.
- Consent orders secure financial agreements and are legally binding. Informal agreements carry no legal protection.
- There is a twenty-week cooling-off period after the application before applying for a conditional order, followed by at least six weeks before the final order is granted.

6

The Kids Are Our Priority: Cooperative Parenting

Even if everything else in your divorce feels like it's falling apart, there's one thing every parent wants to get right: minimising the impact on the children. Get this wrong and we worry our kids will be affected not just now but for years to come. We can recover from financial setbacks or buy a different home but our relationship with our children is immediate and precious. So is their childhood.

Most parents are of course aware of this – we want to do what's best for our children, and many will stay in an unhappy marriage to avoid disrupting family life. When a decision to separate is finally made, we might then be wracked with guilt and worry about the effect it will have on everyone in the family. The prospect of not waking up every day under the same roof as our children can also be traumatic, and planning for that eventuality can be incredibly unsettling. I think for most of us it is the hardest part of the divorce process.

This chapter addresses all of these concerns and shows how you can significantly reduce the impact of separation on your children. Note, however, that you will not have ruined your children's lives and chances if you haven't followed or don't follow every piece of advice in this chapter. You need to read this chapter with a healthy dose of self-compassion and the attitude that if you can do some of this stuff some of the time, you are, in the words of the famous paediatrician and a psychoanalyst Donald W. Winnicott, a 'good enough parent'.

The encouraging news is that research consistently shows that it's not divorce itself that harms children, it's ongoing conflict and the absence of a parent. When handled well, separation can even benefit children by removing them from a high-conflict environment. With effective co-parenting, there's no reason why your children can't continue to thrive and be happy both during and after divorce.

How you co-parent after a separation is of course crucial. This is not about a piece of paper stipulating who has which child when; it's about putting in place a different kind of parenting as you move from being parents who live together to co-parents who live apart, and how you navigate this. That new relationship, now without intimacy, requires new rules and a different set of boundaries. This is a big shift and one that doesn't often get the attention it deserves.

If you get the co-parenting bit right, though – and I'll give you lots of tips on how to do this – the upsides are huge. An amicable divorce or separation greatly increases the chance that you'll co-parent well, so if you need an incentive to stay on course, remind yourself of the following. Recent research – including studies by child clinical psychologist Dr Angharad Rudkin – shows that children who experience positive co-parenting and reduced conflict at home are more likely to have:

- Better emotional well-being both in the short and long term. A positive co-parenting environment promotes a sense of stability, security and trust.
- Higher self-esteem, fewer behavioural problems and lower levels of anxiety and depression.
- Better educational outcomes. When parents are cooperative and involved in their children's education, it creates a stable and conducive learning environment.
- Healthier relationships in the future. Positive co-parenting provides a good model to children, teaching them about cooperation and problem-solving, which will influence their own future relationships and reduce the likelihood of replicating conflict patterns of their own.
- Resilience. Children who witness amicable co-parenting are more likely to develop good coping skills, adapt to change, manage stress and navigate challenges in a more constructive manner. This resilience can benefit them throughout their lives, helping them to face adversity with greater emotional strength.

Many people mistakenly think they need to stay in a dysfunctional relationship for the sake of their children. And yet when I ask parents whether they would advise their children to stay in an unhappy relationship, every time they say, 'No, of course not', despite persisting with their own. It sets a bad example for your children who learn that staying in a bad or unhappy relationship is what adults do. Waiting until children have left home can also have a negative impact on older children. They can feel betrayed, thinking that the relationship between their parents, and by default their own childhood, was a facade or unreal.

Family law

Let's first go over the basics regarding children when you are divorcing or separating. A child in the eyes of the law is someone under the age of 18. In divorce law it extends to when that young person finishes full-time secondary education and financial arrangements can be made until the young person finishes tertiary education (university or college). In real life we sometimes have to take into account older children who live at home beyond this point, but anything legal in this chapter refers to the first two categories (under-18s or those in full-time or in tertiary education). Whilst financial order for children can be made, courts typically will not make 'child arrangement orders' for children over the age of 15 or 16 (which is understandable – have you recently tried to get your 16-year-old to do anything they don't want to do!?).

In general, arrangements, such as where children will live and decisions over schooling, should ideally be made by parents and not by the court. The 'no order principle', a key concept in UK family law, states:

> Where a court is considering whether or not to make one or more orders under this Act with respect to a child, it shall not make the order or any of the orders unless it considers that doing so would be better for the child than making no order at all. *The Children Act 1989, s.1(5)*

In normal speak, this means that unless there is an intractable dispute between parents or a safeguarding issue, matters concerning children should not go to court or be subject to a court order.

The principle that parents, and not judges, are best placed to make decisions for their children was enshrined in the Children Act of 1989. The Act had a lasting impact on how children were treated in divorce and separation cases in general, principally by putting their welfare at the heart of all decisions. It placed an emphasis on 'parental responsibility' – that parents have a legal responsibility to care for their child, regardless of their relationship with the child's other parent – and that children have a right to a relationship with both parents.

Note that both parents retain parental responsibility if they had it during marriage – divorce or separation doesn't change that. A parent cannot voluntarily give up parental responsibility after divorce and it will only be removed by a court in very serious cases of abuse, total absence or adoption.

If you have parental responsibility for a child, you have an obligation to make decisions about their care and upbringing. Important decisions about a child's life – such as where they live and go to school, or giving consent to holidaying abroad – must be agreed with your ex if they have parental responsibility. Day-to-day decisions will be made by the person looking after the child.

Amendments to the language were another change seen in the 1989 Children's Act, in a bid to make the process of divorce and separation less adversarial and more focused on cooperation and the welfare of children. The term 'custody' was dispensed with, as it suggested ownership and control of a child, and replaced with 'lives with' or 'child arrangements'. 'Access' was replaced with 'contact', and there was a move away from parental rights to parental responsibilities. (Despite this, the word 'custody' is still regularly used by couples, perhaps because 'custody battles' and the like are still a feature on TV soaps and dramas.)

As a practical example, in English and Welsh law, instead of saying 'The mother has custody of the child, and the father has access one night in the week and every other weekend', you would say 'The child lives with the mother and has contact with the father one night in the week and every other weekend'.

Of course, shared parenting is far more common these days, thankfully, and it's more likely that children are cared for by both parents more equally. As a result, you'd typically talk about the children living with both parents and setting out an agreed schedule of who and when across a two- or four-week pattern. However you work it, it's a good idea to use the same, up-to-date language and to dispense with all mention of 'custody'!

When it comes to agreeing where a child lives, when and how they will see the other parent and all aspects of their care, you need to try to work with your partner on a parenting plan. (Further details on how to do this and what you should be considering are below. I'll also cover the financial aspects of co-parenting in more detail in Chapter 7.) You can include child maintenance payments and orders for school fees or other financial agreements about children in a consent order, but you don't have to. Many people choose to keep their children's arrangements private and set them out in a parenting plan or co-parenting app, like the *amicable* co-parenting app, where you can record your agreements, bespoke schedules and keep track of expenses and who's paid for what – and whose turn it is to buy the school shoes!

Residence and child arrangements order

Unless there is a major safeguarding issue, the court struggles when it comes to enforcing arrangements with children. If one parent isn't dropping off a child on an agreed day, there's little the court can do other than perhaps take that child away from one of the parents, which probably isn't in the best interests of the child, and therefore unlikely to happen. Far better that you try and sit down with your partner, who is likely to remain in your child's life, and talk through a solution. I appreciate this might be very tricky and desperately unproductive without some third-party help, which is where a mediator can help. There is a range of options to be found, *amicable*'s Separating with Children Service being just one of them (see the Resources section).

Some solicitors might encourage you to include arrangements about your children in a child arrangements order by consent – for a fee of course – but it's not something I advise, given the powerlessness of the court to enforce the order. When it comes to parenting after divorce it's not what is written on a piece of paper that makes the difference but the relationship between you as co-parents. It also strikes me as illogical that on the one hand we have the no order principle, the notion that matters concerning children are not an issue for the court and should be kept private, but on the other the court is quite happy to approve a child arrangements order by consent. You might feel more secure having a piece of paper stamped by the court, but – and I have some experience of this – if someone is determined not to follow the guidance on that piece of paper, then they won't. Before you know it, you might find yourself in a court system that feels designed to make the parenting relationship between you and your ex an impossibility.

As a result, provided it is safe for you to do so, my advice is to find a way to cooperate with your ex when it comes to childcare, even if interaction between you is difficult or very limited. For some parents this will of course be challenging, but the majority find a way, especially if they focus on the well-being of their children and the countless ways in which they will benefit from a really effective co-parenting partnership.

How does co-parenting typically work?

The process of co-parenting usually starts by establishing a detailed parenting plan to outline how exactly responsibilities will be shared after you separate. The plan usually lays out overnight schedules, holiday arrangements, how you will handle special occasions and your agreed parenting values, among many other things.

There are many ways to co-parent and not everyone will decide that equal shared care is right for them. In fact, while 50/50 shared care is growing in popularity between co-parents, the majority, something like 63 per cent of separated families, work out a different split of caring responsibilities. Some might have their child every other weekend with one additional mid-week stay; others might go for weekdays with one parent, weekends with the other.

There are countless other variations, all of which depend on the children's age and needs and the parents' work schedules and living arrangements, and no one size fits all.

It helps to be open to adapting your parenting plan as your child grows older and their needs change. This may involve regular discussions about your child's progress, sharing important information about their education and social life, and agreeing on any rules around bedtimes or screen time.

The goal is to create a consistent and stable environment for your child across both households. This consistency will help them adjust to the new family dynamic while benefiting from the involvement of both parents in their lives.

What are the different types of parenting after separation?

- **Co-parenting.** Parents agree on and apply one set of rules in both homes and make joint decisions about their children. This more consistent approach to routines, rules and expectations can help your child to adjust to the change and minimise stress.
- **Cooperative parenting.** Parents may communicate well and put the children's needs first, even though they don't agree on everything and perhaps have different rules and routines at their respective homes. Both parents are still able to put aside their

personal emotions or grievance when it comes to raising their children.

- **Parallel parenting.** In an ideal world we would all get on super well with our ex-partners but that of course isn't the reality for many separated parents. You may well want to do what's best for your children, but it's impossible for you and your ex to communicate respectfully, perhaps because there's still a lot of anger, hurt and resentment between you. In addition, if there was emotional abuse in the relationship or you need to protect yourself, you may need to keep interaction with your ex to a minimum.

If the above applies to you, it may be that parallel parenting is the best option for you. This is a type of parenting where parents have minimal contact which each other, thereby avoiding situations which can become toxic or negative. This way you also shield your children from any raised voices, door slamming or conflict of any kind. (See page 180 for how to establish a parallel parenting plan.)

How to tell your children about divorce and separation

Before you move ahead with any parenting plan, you obviously need to tell your children that you are divorcing or separating, and this is perhaps one of the hardest parts of splitting up. The thought of doing it can feel daunting and it might feel like there's never a good time to reveal what can be upsetting news. Here are some useful tips from people who've had that difficult conversation.

Get the timing right

It's the six-million-dollar question: when is the right time to tell your child or children? Well, I hate to disappoint you, but there is no perfect time. Procrastinating won't help, but there are some basic guidelines.

It's better to tell children once the decision to separate has been made, not when you're in the early stages of thinking about it. Let them know when something is changing, like spending less time together as a family, putting the house on the market, or one parent moving out. Don't do it before or during exams. Avoid times when one of you will be absent due to a holiday or work commitments. It's usually better to do it in term time so your kids have the additional support of their friends and normal routines ... but as no one size fits all, if they hate or struggle at school then holidays win!

If you can, tell them together, even if they are very different ages, as this will help them and minimise any confusion. Maybe you could give the news at the beginning of a weekend when you are both potentially around and able to answer their questions. This will also give you a chance to talk to them individually afterwards to check their understanding and clarify any issues.

Present a united front

Presenting a united front with your partner when you share the news is often helpful. Doing this together can help your child feel more supported and that you're both still working as a parenting team. Don't blame the other parent – 'Your mum/dad has decided that ...' – as this paints a picture of a powerless victim, and you are not! Your child needs to know you will be okay and you are an equal parent and will make decisions in their best interests – not crumble or defer to the other parent. Your parenting job remains, whatever else is happening in your private life.

Keep it short and simple

Try to present what's happening as a change and not the end of the world. You can acknowledge that the end of a relationship is sad and that change is hard to accept, but while of course things will look different, many things will remain the same. Don't try to dress it up as a good thing, but meet any emotion they feel without judgement and stay focused on their concerns.

The essential message to convey is that you are no longer together as life partners, but you are still together as their parents. The key elements are:

- We love you, and we're sorry our decision is causing you distress
- It's not your fault
- We will both still continue to look after you, but it will be in different houses because we don't get on well enough with each other to want to live in the same house anymore
- We will still be one family, but we will live in two households

Prepare and practise what you are going to say

Agree on what you'll each say to maintain a united message. This helps prevent surprises and keeps things calm. Decide who will speak first and what each of you will say. Have a practice – it's awkward but it's worth it. At *amicable* we help parents prep and practise and test them on questions, which gives confidence when you need it most.

Anticipate questions

Some kids will have many questions right away, while others may need time. Be honest in your answers. If you don't know something, it's okay to say so. Let them know they can ask questions whenever they need to. Common questions might be:

- Why is this happening?
- Why can't you just get on?
- Is this my fault (because I did X or said Y, or because Z happened)?
- Where will I live?
- Where will Mum/Dad live?
- Will I go to the same school?

Manage your own emotions

Think about how you will both react when you give the news. If you are calm when you tell your child, they will have less anxiety. However, it's okay to become upset; it's normal. If you get upset, be kind to yourself. If your child's other parent gets upset, be kind and supportive. You can still be caring towards one another, and this will provide a positive example for your child. If you or your ex have said something bitter about the other within earshot of your children, then it's never too late to apologise and try to fix that. You could say to your child: 'I'm sorry. I shouldn't have spoken like that about Mum/Dad. I'm feeling cross with her/him at the moment, but I understand that you don't want to hear that.'

Don't be surprised by their reactions or lack of them

You may get a strong reaction or no reaction from your children; everything is normal at this early stage. Try to acknowledge and accept their reactions and if they appear to ignore the news or are confrontational about it, try not to be offended. However they react, they will be processing what they have heard in their own way and at their own pace. It might only take them a short time to do this, or it might take a very long time – even into their adulthood.

Children who appear to be cycling through emotions are having a normal response to what is called the 'grief cycle'. Sometimes, children get stuck in one particular emotion or behaviour – anger is a common one, and in younger kids, regressions like bed-wetting can also start to happen more often. This is normal, but if your child is exhibiting an extreme reaction or has been stuck for a while then it's best to get some support from the child's school or a family consultant. It's a tricky balance between being rightly concerned and being overly anxious about a completely normal reaction.

> Parenting expert Sue Atkins has a great tip when it comes to talking to young children about divorce or separation. Take a large sheet of paper and draw a big circle on it. Divide the circle into pieces of pie and work with the kids to write on each segment the things that won't change.
>
> This will give your kids a sense of security and keep the changes from overwhelming them. It can make

> the process of telling kids about divorce a lot easier on everyone as it stops the idea of 'total system breakdown' from entering your child's mind.

Case study: A letter

One of our divorce specialists worked with a couple on how to tell their two boys, aged 9 and 11, about their decision to separate. They had prepared a letter they were going to give to the boys after the conversation, which we thought was excellent. They also shared the letter with the wider family and school just so everyone was on board about how they were going about this.

In our family we have a number of different relationships between all of us. You two have a relationship with each other, and you both have a relationship with each of us, your parents. Mum and Dad also have a relationship with each other.

For some time now, Mum and Dad have felt that our relationship needs to change – not the one that we have with either of you, but the one that we have with each other.

We are still friends, but we do not want to continue being married. This has nothing to do with either of you but is our decision about what is right between us.

We do not regret our marriage, and we have had some great times, and of course, we have had you two – which is the best thing ever.

We have decided to change things so that we can both be happier and concentrate on being the best Mum and Dad to both of you.

Mum has found an amazing house that she will be living in and you will be able to spend time with her there. Dad will stay living in this house.

We also want to do some family things all together: Dad's famous roast dinners from time to time, Christmas – and maybe other things that will come along. We will always make sure to both come to important things like parents' evening and sports matches.

We love you both very much and we know that this is a big announcement and you will have lots of questions over the next few weeks. Do you have any now?

Teenagers

If you have teenagers or older children, you'll obviously need to tell your news in a different way. As they are older, they will be better able to process complex information, so treat them with respect and honesty when talking about divorce or separation. Where possible, be direct about the situation, acknowledging the complexities of adult relationships while avoiding placing blame.

Bear in mind that teenagers may have strong opinions and emotions, so encourage them to share their thoughts and feelings during the conversation. Listen to what they say and make them feel heard. Be prepared for a range of reactions, from anger to sadness, to advice-giving or even indifference – this may change with time as the news sinks in.

Teen brains are still developing and are prone to black-and-white or all-or-nothing thinking. This means their reactions can sometimes be quite harsh and – let's be honest – 'judgy'. The key is to give them space to express themselves and listen – letting them air their views does not mean you agree with them. Silence can be your best friend and a powerful tool – and making it clear to the other parent that this is your strategy is a good plan. Sometimes the other parent may expect you to counter or defend against what's being levelled at you, so having a clear communication strategy is important to avoid misunderstandings between the two of you.

Parenting plan

A parenting plan is a written agreement made by parents about how they will co-parent their children after separation or divorce. It carries no legal weight but it's a document that acts as a guide and should be revised as your children grow older or circumstances change.

It can help you to think about what your children need and what is important for them, all of which can be difficult if you're going through your own emotional struggles.

A parenting plan can help you set priorities and give structure for future life, which may feel uncertain right now. It also means you are thinking about things in the cold light of day – not in the hot ire of a disagreement!

You can create your own parenting plan or download *amicable*'s free one where you can input schedules and events, communicate with your ex, manage expenses relating to childcare and set goals so you remain focused on the future. See the Resources section for a link to our parenting plan.

Things you need to consider in a parenting plan

Parenting goals. Think about what your children need to thrive and be happy. Are you going to have your own rules when you see the children or are you going to parent with a common set of rules? Remember there are no right and wrong answers, just what works for your children and for you as parents.

Living arrangements. Getting the basic arrangements in place quickly is an important step that parents can take to minimise the long-term impact on children. There are many different shared-care patterns you can choose for your family and you should agree on what works for the children as they age. You could ask for their thoughts but be clear you are the adults so you will make the decision.

Questions to consider:

- Where will we and the kids live? How close together do we need to be to minimise travel time?
- How will we share the care – e.g. a 50/50 split, or something else?
- What pattern of days works best: week on week off, 2, 2, 5, 5, or something different?
- Who will look after the kids when we can't – e.g. grandparents, friends, babysitters, a shared nanny?
- How will pick-ups and drops-offs work?

School holidays. Children have lots of holiday throughout the year, at least thirteen weeks in the UK, so you need to think about how you will cover care. If you share care on a 50/50 split, you both need to be available during the holidays and not assume the other parent will cover it, as you might have done in the past. You may need to work fewer hours in the holidays or decide how you will pay for holiday clubs or additional care.

Trips away. Think about how much holiday away from the home you may have with the children. How will you agree dates for this, and where will the passports be kept? Note that if you take your children abroad and you share parental responsibility with your ex-partner, the law requires that you get written consent from the other parent before going, even for a short holiday. This can be an email, text or letter and must be done whether or not your child lives with you most of the time. If you have a residency order – such as a 'lives with order' – you can take your child away for up to twenty-eight days without the other parent's permission. If you cannot agree, you may need to apply for a 'specific issues order' or 'prohibitive steps order' from the court.

Birthdays and special occasions. Some holidays, such as Christmas, can be an emotional time when you both want to be with your children. There are lots of options for dividing these special occasions – be sure to always put the children's needs and wants first (within reason!). Think about what arrangements you'll put in place for holidays like Christmas, other religious celebration days such as Eid, Diwali and Hanukkah, birthdays, and Mother's and Father's Day.

Health. How will you manage routine dentist, optician and doctor's appointments? How will you share medical information and prescriptions, deal with emergencies and make decisions about your children's healthcare?

Education. You will need to inform your children's school(s) about your separation and give them up-to-date addresses and contact information. How will you oversee homework and organise attending parents' evening, sports days and other events? How will you agree on any new schools and who will pay for school meals and activities?

Child maintenance. All parents have a responsibility to support their child financially, even if they don't see them. Child maintenance is usually a regular monthly payment paid to the parent who cares for the child more or most of the time (see the next chapter for further information on this).

Values, beliefs and behaviours. As your children will be living in different homes, you'll need to think about whether you want to apply similar house rules, such as phone/screen time, expectations over behaviour/manners and whether certain religions or cultural traditions will be upheld in both homes.

> ### Case study: 'Your father doesn't love you'
> *At amicable, we interviewed some people about their experience of divorce when they were children. They shared how divorce has impacted them throughout their lives and the advice they wish their parents had received. Here Nic (aged 62) talks about his experience.*
>
> Mine was a typical childhood of the 1970s. My parents separated when I was around the age of six and I didn't understand what was going on.
>
> The reality of the situation was that both my brother and I were weaponised in the divorce. I didn't have much contact with my father at the time so there was one side of the story and the narrative from my mother

was, well, your father doesn't love you and that's why he left. That's of course a shocking thing to do – a child's logic, especially when I was that age, was okay, yes, my father doesn't love me and that's why he left. It was an incredibly confusing time …

You don't need a licence to have children and yet it's the probably one of the most important things that any human can do. And actually divorce can be a positive thing and you can end up with two sets of parents, if your parents remarry. And if it's done well, it can be a power for good.

But ultimately if you've going to get divorced you've got to start with the children – it's the most important thing.

Tips on effective co-parenting and creating boundaries

Co-parenting is completely different to parenting as a couple. Your relationship with your ex has changed and you are very much in uncharted waters without the proverbial paddle – it can be scary stuff. Here are some tips on how to navigate effective co-parenting and how to set clear boundaries so you and your ex-partner can create a stable and supportive environment for your children while living apart.

Define your new co-parenting relationship – don't attempt to pick up where you left off

Your relationship as partners has ended but your parenting relationship continues, just on a different footing. It's no longer appropriate to have your old intimacies and it's time to redefine the boundaries. When communicating, aim for polite, calm, respectful and neutral. Make proposals, not demands, and start conversations positively by asking for your co-parent's opinions.

I advise parents to think of co-parenting as more of a business/co-worker relationship. How would you express things with them? You might not get as cross or annoyed, and there would be certain things you wouldn't say. You're now on a professional footing and need to be conscious about how you speak to each other in front of the children and model cooperation.

Complete control is not an option – don't sweat the small stuff

You may feel frustrated that your ex does things differently to you or even feel the children are upset by the differences. Avoid spending time and energy on trying to control a situation or what your ex does. Instead, find a time and place to discuss how you both want to parent, look for similarities and agree on some basic house rules around bedtimes, homework routine and discipline.

Stick to your parenting plan

Sticking to a jointly agreed parenting plan is vital for creating consistency and stability for your child. A parenting plan serves as a road map, outlining responsibilities, schedules and expectations for both parents. Following it closely helps children feel secure, knowing that their routines and relationships are being prioritised, even when living in two separate homes.

Keep each other in the loop

To make sure that your child's day-to-day life runs smoothly while living in two separate homes, it's important that both co-parents try to stick to agreed timings or let each other know of any changes to the plan.

Other logistical details such as what clothing or equipment may be required for school or home activities should also be shared to avoid stress for your child or tension between you as co-parents.

Be flexible

Being flexible with your co-parent when challenges arise shows a willingness to cooperate. While sticking to a parenting schedule is important for consistency, a rigid approach can lead to unnecessary tension.

Flexibility allows both parents to accommodate each other's responsibilities and commitments. It also ensures you are always putting your child first. For example, illness may mean you need to change their overnight schedule for one week. This also sets a good example for your child, demonstrating compromise and teamwork.

Make clear financial commitments

Financial disagreements are one of the most common sources of conflict in co-parenting. To avoid misunderstandings and ensure your child's needs are being met, it's best to clearly define financial responsibilities from the outset. This includes agreeing how you will pay for food, clothing, school resources, medical care, extracurricular activities and any other expenses that contribute to your child's well-being (more on this in the next chapter).

Encourage relationships with extended family

Your children will benefit from having strong relationships with both of you, as well as your extended families. Grandparents, aunts, uncles and cousins can give additional support, love and a sense of identity and offer different perspectives as your children grow up. Encouraging these bonds means allowing your child to spend time with extended family members on both sides, even if you have personal differences with them.

Encouraging your child to feel part of this larger support network can boost their emotional well-being and resilience.

Seek help

When you can't overcome disagreements yourselves, it's important to recognise that outside support is needed. Professional support such as *amicable*'s Separating with Children Service, mediation or counselling can provide a neutral environment where both parents can communicate openly and work towards solutions that prioritise the best interests of their child.

Co-parenting specialists and mediators are trained to facilitate discussions, helping parents navigate complex issues such as financial arrangements and parenting approaches. Counselling can also address deeper emotional challenges that might be affecting the co-parenting relationship.

Navigating parallel parenting

If communication, cooperation or trusting your partner is difficult, or there's a history of abuse, then you may need to adopt a parallel parenting strategy. Rather than talking, you might communicate via text messages in a co-parenting app or make decisions via email.

Sometimes when issues have had to be settled through proceedings in the family court, a judge might mandate the use of an app like *amicable*'s co-parenting app. In this scenario or if you just have very different parenting ideas, it's likely you'll have varying rules and routines in each home. That might not be ideal, but children can adapt and often understand that different settings like school or home have different rules. It's a bit like if they visit their grandparents, they know they should sit at the table to eat dinner or shouldn't jump on the sofa – rules that become normal for them. So long as the rules are consistent and your children feel loved and secure then they will be okay.

Similarly, once you and your ex have agreed your parenting plan – such as which days the kids will be in each home, school drop-offs, etc. – it's likely those agreements will be more fixed. As there's less communication, there's less deviation from those plans, which some children respond well to as they know where they will be on any given day or time.

Many people start with parallel parenting or cooperative parenting but find that communication with their ex improves, which can gradually lead to a loosening-up of the rules. That shift is often driven by one partner doing something kind without expecting anything in return. If you and your ex-partner are stuck in a tit-for-tat mode – 'If you can't pick the kids up on Thursday, then I'm not going to drop them off on Sunday' – relations or arrangements between you will never move on. Your world is still being defined by your ex's behaviour and actions and you're reliant on them doing the right thing.

The key is to take a step back and detach yourself from what your ex does. You might let the kids be with their mother on Mother's Day (even if it's your weekend) but you might not see them on Father's Day in return because it's Mum's weekend and she's made plans – it's not ideal but you've accepted the situation. You know you're doing the right thing – which is great modelling for the kids – and what you're doing is not predicated on your ex doing the right thing. If you reach this stage – and I really understand how tough that is to do – it's a good sign you're recovering and emotionally moving on from the divorce.

How to establish a parallel parenting plan in five steps

- **Step 1:** Determine your agreed plan or where the kids will be between the households. Set up a diary or use an app that clearly shows where they will be sleeping for their school routine and establish plans for holidays and celebrations.
- **Step 2:** Determine the boundaries of start and finish times and how the children will be dropped off and collected. Be specific about times to avoid confusion.
- **Step 3:** Establish the location of drop-offs and collections. To minimise communication at drop-offs and collections, choose neutral places or places

where the children feel comfortable to switch cars. Remember they will have clothing and possessions to manage as well.

- **Step 4:** Have a plan for cancellations or changes. These will happen for all sorts of reasons, and you should both be clear about the way you should address this. It's never a good idea to try and thrash this stuff out at the next handover! Also, be very clear if the cancelled time can be made up at a later date and when.
- **Step 5:** Have an agreed way to handle any disputes that may arise. No plan is 100 per cent perfect and there is no foolproof step-by-step guide for how to parallel parent. So, if you find yourself being drawn into a hostile conversation, shut it down and seek professional help.

Co-parenting teenagers

Divorce is challenging for all children regardless of their age, but it can be particularly difficult for teenagers. They are already going through an enormous period of change in their lives and having two parents who are at odds with one another can exacerbate this.

Tips to help co-parent your teenager

Don't discuss the details of your separation with your teenager. A common mistake is treating your teenager like a friend rather than your child. This can be tricky as your child gets older – but while teenagers are more mature and independent than younger children, they don't need to know the ins and outs of your divorce or separation. Giving them too many details or over-sharing is putting unfair responsibility on them and may warp how they feel about their other parent.

Actively support your teenager's relationship with their other parent. Don't be neutral, be positive – it's important that your children spend time and build a relationship with each of you. This can be difficult to manage with a teenager, but by helping them to connect with their other parent, you will be assisting them through the challenge of separation and divorce.

Don't be surprised if they don't want to talk to you. Sometimes your teens won't want to reveal how they are feeling – perhaps because they don't want to upset you, or they would prefer to talk to someone more removed from the situation, or they want to resolve things their own way.

At *amicable* we have collected material for an AI chat bot – Yuni – on our Split Happens platform, where young people aged 13 to 30 can ask questions about their parents' separation. It's safer than using the internet or a standard AI tool because we've curated all the material and removed the possibility of dangerous content coming up. It gives proper advice and can show how to handle complex emotional situations in a safe and therapeutic environment. See the Resources section for a link to Split Happens.

What to watch out for

There's no single way that children and young people respond and react to the news that you and their other parent are divorcing or separating. Each child is different and the family circumstances and dynamics will dictate their response. You know your child better than anyone so look out for drastic changes in behaviour. It's natural for children to act out, or distance themselves for a while, especially when their parents are going through a separation or divorce, but it's important to try to make sure that this doesn't impact them long term. The trick is to work out what's temporary or 'normal teen behaviour' versus signs that something is wrong.

Some warning signs that your divorce/separation may be impacting your teen:

- **Education:** if their grades or behaviour in school are negatively impacted
- **Mental health:** if they seem overly stressed, reserved, depressed or anxious
- **Relationships with others:** they don't see their other parent, they are falling out with friends and/or family, or entering into unhealthy relationships
- **Risky behaviour:** they start using illegal substances and/or engaging in underage sexual activity, or you see an escalation in their risk taking

Of course, all of the above can be attributed to the natural rhythm of teenage years, but if you find yourself very worried about your teenager's behaviour and you think your divorce or separation is negatively affecting them in a pronounced way, it's important to seek external help such as therapy, counselling or medical advice. Before you do, talk to your teenager first as they may resent it if you go ahead and arrange things or speak to people without their knowledge. It's a good idea to give your teen the option of getting their own help, but if they refuse you can step in.

Case study: Bolt from the blue
Alex's parents separated when she had just started university. Now aged 35, she talks about the impact it had on her.

My parents separated when I was 18, a couple of months into my first year of university, and it really came as a bolt from the blue. I hadn't anticipated it up until that time – I definitely was one of those people who thought they had the perfect family.

It impacted me tremendously. It was definitely led by my dad, which was really difficult for me as well as I had previously worshipped my dad, and we had a close relationship – we're very similar – and I found it difficult to view things positively.

It made me look back and question everything I had known before. For a long time I very much railed against the idea of long-term relationships, and marriage, and having children myself because I assumed it would all fail.

In summary

- Children's well-being is related to reduced conflict, not the divorce itself. An effective co-parenting approach can protect them and model healthy relationships for the future.
- Co-parenting can work in many different ways. From cooperative to parallel parenting, the key is finding the approach that fits your situation. Shielding children from conflict, even if this means minimal contact between parents, can still provide stability and love.
- Acknowledge the shift from partners to co-parents with new boundaries. Treat it more like a professional partnership: polite, calm, and focused on joint decision-making in the children's best interests.
- A clear, flexible parenting plan is essential. Plans create security for children, but they must also evolve as children grow older and circumstances change.
- Communication matters. Keep each other informed about practical details and avoid speaking negatively about one another. Present a united front and reassure your children of your continued love and care.

7

School Shoes and Smartphones: Who Pays for the Children?

When a relationship ends, ensuring the financial arrangements of any children involved becomes one of the most important – and often most sensitive – tasks for separating parents. This chapter will guide you through the key considerations, including how to work out child maintenance, the responsibilities of parents, and how to reach a fair and workable agreement that supports your child's future.

Both parents are legally responsible to support their children financially, regardless of who the children live with. This applies even if the parents are not married or if one parent does not see their children. Child maintenance is the regular financial support paid by the parent who does not live with the child most of the time (or as much as the other parent). The amount is based on where the children live, how much time the children spend with the non-resident (paying) parent after separation, and, of course, the financial resources of the paying parent and whether the paying parent has other children (s)he is supporting.

There are four main ways of arranging financial support for children. The most common and preferred method is to make a private arrangement with your partner about how to cover your children's living costs. Alternatively, you can include agreements about child maintenance in a consent order. Or, if you and your ex can't agree, you have two further options: if your case is going before a judge and is in the court process, the judge can order the amount of child maintenance; or you can apply to the Child Maintenance Service (CMS) and they will calculate payments – and there is an option to get them to enforce payments.

Calculating child maintenance

When working out how much payments should be, a good starting point is to use the child maintenance calculator found on the government website (**gov.uk/calculate-child-maintenance**). It asks you a series of questions, such as how many children you have, how many nights a week you and your partner will have the children, and how much taxable income the partner paying earns. The figure it comes up with is based on the paying parent's gross income, with reductions based on the number of nights the child stays with them.

Calculations are based on the paying parent's earnings and not what the receiving parent is earning. So, for instance, if your ex is paying you £1,000 a month to cover your child's costs, and you get a pay rise, you still receive

£1,000 from your ex as only the paying parent's earnings are taken into account.

It's also important to note that the child maintenance calculation should be viewed solely as a starting point as it covers only the very basic living costs of looking after a child, such as heating, food and essential clothing. The actual costs of looking after most children are much higher once you factor in childcare costs (such as nursery or after-school clubs), school trips or extracurricular activities, mobile phones or one-off expenses, holidays and travel, additional clothes and other sundries, none of which is covered under the CMS amount.

As a result, once you have your basic CMS figure, you then need to work out what the additional costs are for *your* children by listing them in a spreadsheet or in the *amicable* co-parenting app. At *amicable* we do an audit of what the children's costs are, splitting them into must-haves, important but not obligatory, and optional.

Note that it's easy to underestimate how much we spend on our children, particularly when they are not at school. In England and Wales they are on holiday for at least thirteen weeks a year, during which time we might need to buy in extra food or cover the costs of activities or holiday clubs.

> Possible additional costs, beyond basic child maintenance:
>
> - Childcare or school fees
> - Out-of-school activities, school trips and travel
> - Medical expenses and toiletries
> - Toys and books
> - Mobile phones and computers
> - Holidays
> - Clothing, presents/parties and other extras

Once we have listed all of the additional costs, we also look at the income and outgoings of parents and arrive at an eventual figure to cover payments. That figure varies according to individual circumstances, what people feel is fair and how couples worked their finances prior to separation.

As an example: if you split care exactly 50/50 then you might split costs equally. Or, if one of you has the children two-thirds of the time then they could contribute one third of the cost, and the other parent two-thirds of the cost. Or, you could calculate contributions according to income – if your partner earns twice as much as you, then they might contribute twice as much to the cost.

school shoes and smartphones: who pays for the children?

An *amicable* example

Child maintenance	Salary	No. of nights with children per year
Parent 1, part time	£27,000	261
Parent 2, full time	£96,000	104 (alternate weekends, one mid-week overnight)

Applying the figures above to a family with three children of school age, the statutory child maintenance calculation is £952 per month. This payment is meant to go towards keeping a roof over the children's heads and keeping them fed. In most families the costs are much higher. And it's not until you write it all down that you realise what you spend. This *amicable* example shows how things quickly add up. These three children did a lot of extracurricular activities, and the parents set out a schedule of the costs of these. They were shocked when they added everything up.

PARENTS' SCHEDULE OF CHILDREN'S EXPENSES

Children's expenses (x3 children)	Cost per month	Cost per year
Clothing	£50	£600
Birthdays/Christmas and gifts	£50	£600
Outings and entertainment	£150	£1,800
Books and home entertainment	£10	£120
Travel/fares to school/college	£20	£240
Childcare	£150	£1,800

Children's expenses (x3 children)	Cost per month	Cost per year
School expenses	£30	£360
Lunches	£210	£2,520
Weekly activities	£108.33	£1,299.96
Holiday activities	£250	£3,000
Music lessons	£107.50	£1,290
Pocket money	£60	£720
Tuition	£120	£1,440
Haircuts	£60	£720
Phones	£30	£360
TOTAL	£1,405.83	£16,869.96

Each child had a school activity, a music lesson and out-of-school activity, plus one child was being tutored. All of a sudden it was clear that the statutory amount was not going to cover the children's costs, even if they cut back. The actual cost of the three children was nearly £17,000 a year, or £1,400 a month, in addition to the £952 statutory payment that covered the basics.

These parents decided to split the costs in line with their salaries. Parent 1 paid 25 per cent of the children's expenses and Parent 2 the remaining 75 per cent. This meant an additional £1,054 on top of the statutory payment, so the total Parent 2 paid was £2,006 a month.

My point in using this example is to highlight the difference between what the state mandates you should pay and what you really need to pay for your kids. Of course, the paying parent has to be able to afford the extra otherwise you both (and your

> children) have to cut your cloth accordingly. So when looking at these payments we also looked at Parent 2's outgoings to check the additional payment was affordable. For me, this illustrates one of the key principles of having an amicable divorce, which is doing the right thing rather than simply doing what the law says you must.

There are lots of different ways of working out financial support but the important thing is you discuss it with your partner, take on board what they have to say and ensure they understand your needs and the costs. The objective is that you both feel comfortable with the figures and everyone is clear about the costs involved. I appreciate that in practice these kinds of conversations can be challenging and there's potential for conflict – see below for further tips on this.

Once you've agreed on an amount for child payment, you then must work out the logistics for paying it. Many separated parents retain a joint account for costs relating to children and this might be an option for you. For some a joint account might not be appropriate, for example if you want to keep your finances separate or problems around money or debt contributed to the breakdown of your relationship. You might agree to a one-off monthly payment or, if you're on very good terms, an as-and-when principle. If you have a joint account or use a parenting app that itemises spending, you may need to make allowances for the odd personal item – deodorant or cat food, say – that might be bought alongside stuff for the children.

Remember there may be unforeseen costs and over the long term you need to factor in inflation so the figure you agree will not be set in stone for ever. You'll need to review your financial arrangement at least annually as circumstances change, such as a child going to a new school or if there's a job change.

Agreeing child maintenance with your ex can be difficult, especially if emotions are running high or trust has broken down. With the right approach, however, arguments or conflict can be avoided, especially if you focus on your child's needs. Here are some tips on how to have an amicable discussion about parenting costs and payments.

Prepare before you talk

Write an initial list of all the costs connected with your child, which you can then discuss with your partner. You might need to look back over payments, such as childcare costs, school shoes, etc. Most online banking apps make this less of a chore than it used to be!

Choose a calm, neutral time and place to discuss

If communication between the two of you is difficult, use a mediator, amicable divorce specialist, or liaise via a parenting app, email or text.

What is your partner's attitude to money?

Can you reframe a suggestion so that it helps the situation? How much of a grip did your partner have on the finances or costs when it came to the children – do you need to go through it all slowly or were they more on top of the finances than you were?

Focus on children's needs, not the past relationship

Think about what your child needs in the future – do not dwell on the past or bring up old arguments. Avoid blame or emotional language: 'You never pay the bills', etc. Instead try: 'Can we talk about what's fair for maintenance or what you can realistically contribute …?' And try to stay calm.

Create a simple agreement in writing

This doesn't have to be formal; just write it all down in a parenting plan, app or email. Detail the amount, who pays whom, when, how and how often it will be reviewed. Don't assume a verbal agreement is enough.

Be consistent but open to adjustments

Be consistent with payments but you will need to review them as you go along. We all know that children's expenses change practically every term and there are so many trips and unforeseen expenses that crop up.

The Child Maintenance Service

If you and your partner are unable to agree on costs, or you are having trouble persuading them that they need to pay, you can use the Child Maintenance Service. Note that anyone who has children with another person whom they're not living with anymore can claim child maintenance, whether or not they are getting divorced. To qualify for child maintenance, children must be under the age of 16, or under 20 if they are in full-time approved education or training.

Once you make a formal application to the CMS, they will triage your situation and then make an assessment on what your partner should be paying; although, as mentioned earlier, their calculation will cover only basic costs. The only case where the other partner may not have to pay child maintenance is if they share 50 per cent of the care of their children (but it does have to be consistently 50 per cent) and therefore neither parent is considered the 'non-resident' or 'paying' parent; or they are a full-time student with no income; or they are in prison.

The CMS offers two main ways to handle payments between separated parents:

1. The CMS calculates the amount, and parents arrange payments themselves.
2. The Collect and Pay service, where the CMS collects money from the paying parent and pays it to the receiving parent.

To use the Collect and Pay service, 20 per cent is added to the payment by paying parents, and 4 per cent is deducted from the payment to receiving parents. It strikes me as unreasonable and, frankly, unkind that receiving parents and children should have money taken away from them when it's usually the paying parent who has proved unreliable or has been withholding finances. The situation can be particularly distressing in cases of domestic violence or abuse.

In theory the CMS can force a parent to pay child maintenance and they have the statutory power to take payments from the paying parent's salary and bank account, seize property or take court action, and even revoke passports or driving licences (although the latter is virtually never done). In practice, however, the powers of the CMS are limited, largely because the service is woefully underfunded and understaffed. The system it oversees is very easy to manipulate and many parents get away without paying maintenance. Common tactics include hiding income, especially among those who are self-employed or earning cash in hand. Many parents who don't see their children or who are prevented from doing so, mistakenly believe they are not obliged to pay child maintenance, when in fact they are.

As a result, millions in unpaid maintenance has accumulated, meaning children are going without essentials and homes are being repossessed, making this one of the biggest contributory factors to child poverty in this country. According to the Department for Work and Pensions, 43 per cent of children in single-parent households are in poverty compared to 26 per cent of children in couple households. In the last three months of 2023, 150,000 children – nearly half of the 340,000 children covered by the CMS Collect and Pay Service – received no financial support from absent parents, despite the CMS being responsible for their payment. That's a shocking statistic, and if the CMS were more effective in pursuing payments, they could potentially lift 60 per cent of children of single parents not benefiting from maintenance out of poverty.

The charity Gingerbread, which supports single parents, has led a prominent campaign in the UK to reform the CMS, and as of May 2025 the government has confirmed that such reform will be part of its forthcoming child poverty strategy.

Women after divorce

As nine out of ten single parents are women, mothers are disproportionately affected by the failings of the CMS. In fact, when it comes to divorce in general, research has shown that women on average end up financially worse than their male counterparts. The cost of running two households often means that partners are worse off after separation, but according to recent studies by Legal & General, women on average see their income halved in the year following divorce, while men's incomes fall by 30 per cent in the same period. Nearly double the number of women (19 per cent versus 10 per cent of men) struggle to meet the cost of essentials after divorce, often because many mothers have to reduce their working hours due to childcare responsibilities.

In the long term, women also face financial insecurity. When negotiating a divorce agreement, women often prioritise keeping the family home over securing a share of pensions, a decision that often sees them retiring with significantly smaller pension pots than their male counterparts. The common portrayal of women as 'gold diggers' during divorce belies the financial reality most women face.

Consent order

Child maintenance agreements can also be documented and made legally binding in a consent order. By doing this, if a parent fails to make their payments, the court can enforce them. There's a caveat, though, as the court only has the power to do this for twelve months from the approval of your order. After that, the Child Maintenance Service takes over and if you've agreed a higher than statutory sum in your consent order you may lose out as the CMS then reassesses the maintenance claim and it's likely the calculation will go down. In practice it means you're only protected for a year after your divorce.

As a result, I advise couples to add an agreement in their consent order – known as a 'recital' – stipulating that neither parent will make a claim to the CMS after twelve months. It's not enforceable by the courts but it provides at least a clear record of agreement and can prevent further disputes. It's another reason to stay on good terms and keep things amicable as there's only so much protection you can get from the law! Goodwill and cooperation have a lot more power.

Parents sometimes want to agree on different or more bespoke kinds of payments to cover their children's costs, such as school fees, paying into a trust or agreeing to lump sums or property transfers in lieu of payments. These can all be added to your consent order – but the statutory right to child maintenance cannot be taken away.

However you agree on supporting your children financially, keep their needs front and centre of all your decisions. Remind yourself that their welfare is paramount and that you want to give your children the best possible start in life. In the next chapter we'll take a look at finances in general when a relationship ends.

In summary

- Whatever the circumstances of your separation, both parents remain legally responsible for supporting their children.
- The government's child maintenance covers only basic needs. In reality, most children's lives include many other costs and real security comes when parents cooperate and go beyond the bare minimum.
- Many families choose private agreements or joint accounts to manage payments. Approaches that reflect income, share of care, or fairness to both parents create more sustainable solutions than sticking rigidly to formulas.
- While the CMS has powers to enforce payments, underfunding and loopholes mean too many children miss out on support. Campaigns for reform continue, but for now, goodwill and cooperation between parents remain more effective.

- Formal written agreements are not required (or encouraged) by the court. Recording arrangements through a parenting plan or app adds clarity and protects against disputes. A positive co-parenting relationship is the best 'tool' to help your kids thrive post-divorce.

8

Money, Money, Money

Money is complicated. And it's not just the jargon and the confusing acronyms that can make your head spin, it's also the psychological relationship we have with it. We don't just manage money, we obsess about it, emotionally project onto it or ignore it altogether. It can make us feel anxious, powerful and everything in between. Divorce or separation can amplify those emotions, but acknowledging them – and keeping your focus on long-term goals – can help you and your partner reach a fair and amicable financial agreement.

When you are ending a relationship or marriage, you're usually unravelling your shared financial life. Everything that was once joint – bank accounts, property, debt and savings – has to be separated and sorted out, which can be as emotionally and practically challenging as the break-up itself. It's not just a logical division of numbers or feeding something into a spreadsheet and getting out the answer, it's dealing with how you feel about money and what it represents for you.

The relationship we have with money is set early on – by the age of seven, some studies suggest. Early experiences, such as how your parents talked about it (or avoided talking about it), can affect how you feel about money, especially if it was a source of tension in your childhood home. Throw in different personality types, a few life events and the feeling most of us have of 'if only we had a little bit more ...' and you'll see a range of behaviours when it comes to money. You might associate money with freedom and take pleasure in spending it, or you might see it as a source of security and prefer to save whenever possible. Does a fear of not having money drive you to earn more? Or is your drive rooted in the desire to accumulate as much as you can? And how much is enough?

Where you fall on that spectrum affects how you interact with money, and those habits – good or bad – are the ones you'll bring into a relationship. You and your partner might approach finances in completely different ways, and, over time, that alone can wear down a relationship. Maybe one of you likes to splurge extra cash on a holiday while the other prefers to tuck it away for life's inevitable emergencies, like a broken boiler or unexpected car repairs. Or perhaps you were constantly having to bail out your partner's credit-card debts or overspends, all of which can cause a slow build-up of resentment within a relationship.

When you divorce – whether or not issues over money caused the break-up – you need to disentangle your finances and go through them with a fine-tooth comb. At the same time you may be feeling emotionally raw – think back to the emotional journey of divorce – and you're also bringing those long-held attitudes about money. With all that at play, you then have to make tough decisions about how you divide your finances – and your lives.

To progress with a financial agreement, you need first to look at all income and outgoings and provide full financial disclosure on joint assets including property, savings, debt and investments. If you have always kept a tight rein on your money, this might not be too daunting an exercise, but this might also be the first time you've sat down and examined your finances in such detail, especially if you relied on your partner to do this for you.

Many of us are unaware exactly how much we spend on a monthly basis and going through the details – haircuts or gym memberships, for example – can feel exposing. Similarly, you might feel resentment or shock over some of your partner's spending habits – there is potential for tempers to fray at this emotional time.

Dealing with finances, the terminology, the small print, the dizzying numbers, can also be intimidating, especially if you're unfamiliar with the whole world of money. If you're feeling out of your depth, then be assured you're not alone. The very wealthy tend to be well informed about how to invest their money – advisors fall over themselves to offer them guidance. The majority of people, however, muddle on without any such advice, only to be faced, at a very low point in their lives, with making major decisions about their finances.

Once the finances are laid bare, people can also be quite shocked at what they find. In my experience, couples tend to overestimate what they have in their financial pot – rarely do I hear: 'Oh, I didn't realise we had as much as that in our savings account.' Far more common is: 'Oh, really? I thought we'd saved more than that/paid off more of the mortgage than that.'

The realisation that you have less money or income than you thought, which you now need to split to run two separate households, means of course looking very carefully at what's affordable in the future. I don't know anyone who's been through a divorce and not had to change their spending habits. If you go from one home to two homes it is always more expensive, and you have to recut your cloth accordingly. This may also mean immediate changes to shore up the family finances before you agree on how to split everything. As a result, a divorce or separation is a good time to re-evaluate your spending habits or relationship with money and perhaps you can look at how to make changes. Here are some other challenges you might face:

- You or your partner may have built up debt you haven't told each other about, and there can be quite a lot of shame or guilt attached to that.

- Spending habits can reveal all sorts of secretive behaviour, from gambling debts and adultery to the secret mortgaging of the family home, as happened with one couple I worked with. Discoveries like these can be profoundly impactful, both emotionally and practically. You may have thought you knew roughly what your joint assets were and what to expect in a divorce settlement, only to discover that much of that pot has been wiped out by debt.
- When it comes to the relationship we all have with money, it can be frustrating if you have always been the saver in the relationship, diligently putting money into a pension or a savings account, whereas your partner – who perhaps earned a similar income – chose to spend rather than save. Now that you must split any pot you own, one that perhaps you had been paying into for many years, you might feel understandably resentful.

It is of course perfectly natural for various emotions to surface and you may need to sit with those feelings for a while. Over time try shifting your focus from what has happened in the past to the future – you're now closing a joint chapter, your shared life, and moving on to a new stage. If you were organised with money, you'll take those skills with you into the next stage of your life. If you were less in control of your finances, divorce or separation can also be a kind of wake-up call. It can force you to take a hard look at how you've been living and what you've been avoiding. I promise once you confront this reality it will feel better – but I appreciate it's hard to take the first step in that process. Losing the support or structure of a partner might feel overwhelming at first, but it also gives you a clean slate – you're no longer working with a shared system that may have masked your behaviour. Now you have the chance to redefine your relationship with money on your own terms.

> **Money coach**
>
> It's a good idea to get some help when you are having to re-evaluate your finances and spending habits. Traditionally this has been difficult because financial advice has been the preserve of those with a large sum of money to invest. A number of companies and organisations offer money coaching for everyone, including Octopus Money (the sister company to *amicable*). A money coach can help you set financial goals, make a plan and support you in achieving those goals. After a divorce you'll often have different assets or need to create new budgets, and a money coach can help you with the emotional impact as well as the practical steps and advice. I always encourage couples who have been through the *amicable* process to talk to a money coach. To find out more about Octopus Money, see the Resources section.

When it comes to agreeing finances during a divorce, there are generally two ways of approaching things. You and your ex can make a private, informal agreement, which can cover anything, but as it is not legally binding your partner could, at any point in the future, renegotiate its terms and take the matter to court. Alternatively, and this is something which I strongly advise, you can make a legally binding, final agreement – a consent order. This will reflect the law's principle of fairness and there will be no comeback on either of you.

To make a financial agreement legally binding and final it needs to be approved by the court. If you are cohabiting the laws are very different and practically non-existent – see page 29 – but for now let's go over the law concerning finances and divorce.

English and Welsh law

When you divorce, any legally binding financial agreement you make with your partner is outlined in a consent order, which the court reviews and approves before issuing a final order. The law governing financial orders in divorce cases is set out in the Matrimonial Causes Act 1973. The overarching principle is fairness – that a just outcome is reached for both partners.

While the starting point is a 50/50 split, various factors or needs determine what the split will be and how finances will be separated. These factors are set out in Section 25 of the act, and include the income and earning capacity of each partner, financial needs, obligations and responsibilities, standard of living during the marriage, age, any disabilities, contributions to the wellbeing of the family, provision for retirement, and the needs of any children, which takes priority over everything else. The court has two main objectives when approving financial agreements: firstly, that any children remain in a stable home environment; and secondly, as far as possible to ensure (not always the case when you have children) that financial ties between spouses are severed via the clean break order. Let's go over some of these factors in more detail.

Children

The court's primary concern is the welfare of any children and that they have a stable roof over their heads. Some examples of what a judge takes into consideration when deciding whether your consent order is fair are: where your children will live; who your children will live with; their age, mental and physical health; and their educational costs.

Need

A judge will consider whether one of you has a greater need than the other and therefore should get more than half the assets. This could include whether one of you needs ongoing support, or 'spousal maintenance'. This can mean a departure from an even 50/50 split.

Income and earning capacity

If one of you has stayed at home to raise the children, your earning capacity may be reduced, and you may need a greater share of the assets – especially if you cannot raise a mortgage or pay rent. As another example, one of you may have lost your job. In this case, the court may consider how likely it is that you will find another job at a similar level of salary.

Current or potential assets

The judge will consider whether you have split your property and assets in a fair way. This includes assets that are held in sole names and/or were purchased prior to the marriage. If needs dictate, they should be in the mix as well as those held jointly.

Age and health

Pensions become more important the nearer to the retirement age you are. Age, as well as any long-term health issues, may affect your earning capacity and housing needs. A judge will consider whether you have come to a fair arrangement for both of you in retirement and whether splitting pensions equally is fair if you are of different ages.

Length of marriage

In shorter marriages, 'fair' is more likely to mean taking out what you put in – i.e. what you brought to the marriage or civil partnership. Most people agree a marriage of less than two years is likely to lead to this kind of settlement. However, if you have children, the needs of the children will always be prioritised over the length of the marriage.

Contributions made

The law considers financial contributions as equal to those of homemaking (time spent looking after the family). Marriage is a partnership of equals, and the law seeks to distribute assets in a way that recognises this. So, a smaller financial contribution doesn't necessarily mean less of the assets.

A fair financial agreement means working out a way to split your money, assets and debts so that you can both move on and manage on your own after the divorce. At a very basic level the court needs to be satisfied that each partner (i) is housed, (ii) has enough money to live on day to day and (iii) has a retirement plan.

Game theory versus goals

To reach a fair agreement with your partner, you need to sort through your finances, work out what you have to split, and consider how to do this fairly. It makes for a challenging conversation.

To help with this difficult process, we use the GROW method ('Goals', 'Reality', 'Options' and 'Way forward') to help people consider their options, make decisions and get a desired outcome based on the reality of their current situation. GROW originated as a coaching framework but its goal-oriented focus works well in divorce negotiation, particularly with couples who want to make their own decisions and work amicably.

When it comes to negotiating finances, lawyers often aim to get the best possible deal for their clients. They want to 'win' the conversation and optimise the position of their client. One person's gain means another person's loss – and of course in a divorce that other person is either you or your partner.

This type of game theory negotiation – a zero-sum, 'if I win, you lose' scenario – is something I avoid when working with couples not just because it often quickly escalates into conflict but also because it invariably fails to achieve the best results for them. If you come at the negotiation from a different perspective and focus on what each person actually *wants*, what is important to them, you are creating the potential for more of a win-win situation, where each person gets more of what they want.

Economists have been writing about this type of negotiation for decades, but the best way to describe the value/goal-based negotiation is with the following example:

> *Two children are arguing over an orange. They both want the orange, so their mother says, well, I can cut the orange in two and you can have half each. She does this and each child ends up with half an orange and half of what they wanted. It turns out that one child just wanted the peel to bake a cake, while the other wanted to eat the flesh. They had missed the opportunity of having 100 per cent of what they wanted. Had the mother understood why they wanted the orange or what was important to them they could have each had what they wanted in more of a win-win solution.*

Obviously, divorce is not that simple but it's a useful analogy to get people thinking about why negotiating in a goal-based way – what is your goal, what is important to you and why – can make a lot of sense. You can't come away with everything in divorce negotiations, but if you rank what's most important to you, you have a better chance of getting more of what you want rather than half of what you don't want.

The theory (and it's complicated, so I suggest you read *Game Theory and the Transformation of Family Law* by Kenneth H. Waldron and Allan R. Koritzinsky if you want to understand the maths!) says it's possible for you each to walk away with 73 per cent of what you want, rather than the 50/50 split of a traditional horse trade.

It works because individuals often have different wants and needs. In my experience, women often rank keeping the family home over investments or pensions, whereas men might place more priority on building back wealth. There can be issues with this solution – one partner keeps the home, the other any investments – but it demonstrates in real terms the kind of conversations we have, in which we ask couples to rank what's important to them and to frame this through goal-setting.

To divorce amicably, couples make their own decisions about how to split their finances and my job is to talk through some of their assumptions and ensure they've thought everything through. You might have a good idea of what your needs are right now but what about when you retire or when the children have left home – what will that look like, and will your needs be met then? You might think now that downsizing when you retire sounds okay, but this could mean moving out of your home and living on a much smaller income – have you really thought that through? So, it's a question of thinking through your finances in both the short and the long term. Divorce won't sort your finances for the rest of your life, as that's an ongoing process, but getting to grips with your situation and establishing some financial security will build a firm foundation.

GROW

Let's take a closer look at the GROW process, which ensures that both partners are clear about their financial situation, their goals and the options available to them.

The goals session is something I do with couples right from the outset, working with both partners together, unlike mediators who will first talk to people individually. I avoid this as I think it's important that we discuss the ground rules first, including how best to communicate. Individual conversations can be important in getting people over the line, but I like to make sure couples talk openly about their goals from the get-go, without taking 'positions'. I also find that if couples can manage the first goals sessions, it's a good indicator the GROW method will work for them. Here are the kinds of issues and questions we discuss as part of the GROW framework.

G is for GOALS

Think about what you want your life to look like after the divorce. It doesn't have to be money related; just consider the broad picture once the dust has settled and you've moved on to the next stage of your life. The kinds of goals or aspirations you might discuss with your partner could be:

- Where will you live?
- What kind of relationship do you want with your former partner?
- What are your hopes for your children?
- How much time do you want to spend with your children?
- Are you going to work?
- When will you retire and what will that look like?

The idea is to choose three or four goals each. These might be shared goals – perhaps you both want to co-parent, sharing childcare as equally as possible, and you have similar aspirations for your children.

You might also have different goals – perhaps your partner wants to sell the family home, whereas you want to stay in it. That's fine too, because the point of this exercise is to set out what's important to you or your partner and to think about those goals from an interest/values point of view rather than what your 'position' is ('The only option is to do XYZ, and I'm not going to budge on that').

If you were going down the lawyer route a solicitor may well set out a legal case as to why their client should be entitled to stay in the family home or take their money out, based on the law or case law to support this position. *amicable* on the other hand would ask this question – okay, you want to sell your house, but let's explore why? We'd want to understand the true 'interest' in the desire to sell. Your partner might say it's about the money – it's better if we settle now and each take our money as soon as we can.

At that point I might explain that there could be ways of releasing money or achieving the financial aim without selling the house. Once that's clarified, it might become apparent that your partner's goal of selling the house has nothing to do with money. There's an emotional reason – it's about the fact that they are leaving while you and perhaps the rest of the family are staying, and the thought of that is upsetting.

The conversation might then pivot to address that emotional need. You might work out a solution where your partner still has a connection to the home in some way or you help them set up their house so it feels homely and like a place they want to be with the children. Or perhaps you sell the family home because now you understand what the underlying issues are and you might be more open to exploring an alternative solution. No one is trying to 'win' – you're just weighing up options that work for both of you and for your family. But having a solid set of goals is important (we will return to goals when we are deciding the 'way forward' – the W of GROW).

> ### Case study: How GROW can work
> *Here one of our divorce specialists described how the GROW method worked for one couple, where it seemed they might never agree but were able to talk through options, make decisions for themselves and eventually achieve a full financial agreement.*

At our first goals session, I thought there was no way they were ever going to come to an agreement because the wife looked so down and talked very little. She was the lower earner of the two and the husband had cheated on her so it was very difficult between them.

Her goals were very focused on the children and feeling secure and not wanting to upend her life because of what 'he' had done. The husband's goals were about holding on to as much cash, investments and pension as he could so he could start a new life with his new girlfriend. I spent time with them both, really getting underneath what they wanted and trying to keep the wife focused on the future. I didn't want to allow what had happened to drive negotiations or for the husband to abandon his family in his rush to move forward. It's so hard in these situations, but the court doesn't award more in a settlement because of the other person's behaviour. And however blinded by love you are in the moment, you will always be a family member and in all likelihood you will want and need to be part of your children's lives.

The breakthroughs came when we were going through financial disclosure and options. Taking the wife through it all step by step and helping her take control changed everything. She was able to envisage her future life, to believe in her own abilities, and this made it easier for her to say what she needed as opposed to refusing to accept any changes at the outset. Once the husband could see she was actively engaged and meeting him with ideas, he was way more forthcoming with what he was able to accept. I think he had more respect for her.

We're now on session four and they've come to a full agreement! The wife has changed into a different person, she looks so much better and well in herself – it's a complete transformation!

> ## Fight, flight, freeze or fawn?
>
> When money is tied up with fear or past wounds, our nervous system can shape how we respond to issues over money. Here are some common reactions:
>
> FIGHT – obsessing over every penny, spreadsheets and everything in between.
>
> FLIGHT – moving out without discussion, being hard to pin down, and then making decisions without consultation.
>
> FREEZE – paralysed into inaction, leaving emails or letters unopened.
>
> FAWN – people-pleasing, agreeing to unfair settlements just to keep the peace.
>
> But being amicable isn't about giving in. True amicability means having the hard, honest conversations so that both people's needs are properly met.

R is for REALITY

Once you've discussed your goals, you and your partner then need to provide a full, honest account of your financial situation, known as a financial disclosure. You both must have a clear understanding of what money or assets you have and where it is before you divide it. By doing this, you're laying out the reality of your financial situation.

Being open and honest about your finances is not only a prerequisite to a good financial separation but a legal requirement. You will need to sign a statement of truth when you submit your financial disclosure, confirming that you've made a 'full, frank and honest disclosure' and the details are complete and accurate. You should have evidence for everything you disclose and be able to show it to your partner before you can both sign the statement of truth.

On the gov.uk website there is a long and detailed form – Form E – which you can use for your financial disclosure. It's twenty-eight pages long, though once you add the required supporting documents, the full bundle is usually much larger. The size and complexity of it can reduce people to tears (me included) and it's often described as 'intimidating' and 'overwhelming'. If you are using a solicitor who is acting on your behalf, or you are part of contested court proceedings, you will need to fill in a Form E. They will charge you by the six-minute interval for checking your form and interrogating your partner's form – a part of the process where you can rack up high costs. You can, however, avoid this if you establish good communication and an understanding of what is legally required.

Despite what many solicitors tell you, if you are using an alternative legal service like *amicable*, it is not a legal requirement to fill in a Form E. To sign the statement of truth you must be happy that you and your partner both know what the complete financial picture is between you – and how you achieve this is up to you.

As an alternative to Form E, *amicable* has designed a simple to use, informative online form for the financial disclosure. You and your partner can each fill in your own forms – you can nominate which one of you will complete joint information (jointly held assets) so you don't have to duplicate work – and it's a fully transparent secure system so you can see what's being inputted by each other. It guides you through all the steps, providing you with drop-down explanations as you go along, ensuring you don't forget anything and resulting in a far less traumatic experience than the dreaded Form E.

For the financial disclosure you need to detail everything you own jointly or individually, irrespective of whether you think you are going to split them, or whether you feel they are pre-marital. At the very least you should record this in an agreed spreadsheet. These generally fall into the following groups:

- Money in bank and savings accounts
- Property value and mortgage details
- Cars/vehicles
- Salaries and bonuses
- Investments
- Dividends and any other income
- Debt, including credit cards, loans or hire-purchase
- Pensions
- Life insurance policies
- Business details, including cash in business account
- Assets over £500 (jewellery, dowries, watches, etc.)

Your disclosure must also include income, assets or debt held outside of the UK, such as holiday homes, rentals, overseas bank accounts and pension funds.

It's important to note that there is another form on the gov.uk website that often causes confusion when it comes to disclosing assets and applying for a consent order – the D81, 'Statement of Information' (see the Resources section). The D81 is a short summary of your financial disclosure and shows your position now (at the point of divorce) and your position after the divorce if the court were to approve your order. People often think that once they've filled out the D81 Statement of Information form, that's the job done and they don't need to do any more. The government website is not very clear on this – you still need to send a consent order, a completed Form A and the completed D81 for the court to approve your financial agreement.

A D81 is not a substitute for thoroughly disclosing all your assets. The high-level information on the D81 means a judge will only see a summary of your financial position – not the details – and unless you are in contested proceedings the court will not see any evidence of your disclosure, just your statement of truth saying you have disclosed everything.

Property

When you separate, deciding what to do with property can feel daunting, especially when the family home is at the heart of discussions. The first step is to gather all the key information about your property or properties. This includes knowing what each property is worth, whether it is owned outright or mortgaged, and whether there are any early repayment penalties. You should also check whose names are on the deeds and whether you own the property as 'joint tenants' or 'tenants in common'.

Your home is usually the biggest asset to value and there are a couple of main ways to do this. Again, this is where being amicable pays! You can of course pay for a RICS (Royal Institution of Chartered Surveyors) accredited surveyor to value your property. This will result in what is called a 'Red Book valuation' and is a formal property valuation prepared in accordance with the RICS 'Red Book' standards. It sets out the market value of a property in a clear, standardised and court-accepted format. It will therefore cost you money (several hundred pounds).

A more amicable alternative is to invite at least three estate agents to value the property and take the average of their valuations. To avoid bias (for example, if one partner wants a higher value because the other is buying them out), choose the estate agents carefully and use the median (middle valuation when placed in order) or mode (most common valuation) rather than the mean (adding up the valuations and dividing by the number of valuations), as more extreme valuations may skew the results. Alternatively, you could do some desk research, looking at online property sites and coming up with a figure you agree between you.

Note, however, that when it comes to property, agreements in financial orders are usually expressed in terms of a percentage – for example, you split the net proceeds of a sale 50/50 – so the valuation is more of a guide price to help you understand what you might be getting if the property sells.

Pensions

To work out how you are going to split pensions you need to know the value of your pensions – and it can be tricky remembering (and finding) all your old pensions if you've had several jobs! The gov.uk website has a pension finder service – **gov.uk/find-pension-contact-details** – or a quick Google search will throw up other similar services.

Once you've made a list of all your pensions, you can obtain a pension valuation by requesting from your pension provider a cash equivalent transfer value (CETV; sometimes the T is missed out, but it's the same thing!), which calculates how much your pension is worth if you were to transfer it out. It's important to note that there are different kinds of pensions and how accurate the CETV is will depend on what type of pension you have. For example, a CETV may undercalculate some public sector pensions, such as NHS, armed forces or civil service schemes. This is also the case with defined benefit (final salary) plans, which tend to be more valuable than the more common defined contribution plans. If you have those types of pensions or even a mix then it's advisable to get some expert pension advice. There are different types of help available, ranging from actuaries to PODEs (pension on divorce experts).

An actuary report usually costs between £1,000 and £2,000 plus VAT, although *amicable*, through Octopus Money, can now provide a more cost-effective report. See the Resources section for more information.

You should consider getting expert help if:

- The combined CETVs of your and your ex's pensions add up to more than £100,000
- Either of you has one (or more) defined benefit pensions valued at over £100,000

- Either of you has a defined contribution pension with extra benefits
- There is a significant age gap between the two of you
- One of you has a uniformed service pension
- You are considering offsetting; especially if the pension involved is a defined benefit pension
- One of you has a serious medical condition
- There is a choice of pensions to share

Business

If you or your ex-partner owns a business, this can add another layer of complexity to your divorce settlement. Business assets can be difficult to value, and there are many factors to consider when deciding how to divide them fairly. On the other hand, there is a danger of over-complicating things if businesses are sole traders or limited companies set up to pay consulting salaries. These businesses tend to hold little residual value (apart from funds in a bank account, a van or similar) and are set up to facilitate work – if the individual who runs them stopped working there would be nothing left. Those businesses are usually considered to have a 'nil value', requiring only the bank account and vehicle to be disclosed.

If your business is more complex and established and one or both of you believes it has a value, then you'll need specialist help to value your business. There might be multiple shareholders or no obvious way of realising the value of the business, or perhaps you disagree on how valuable it is. There are various methods to value a business – from an assets-based calculation to ones based on future income – all of which come up with very different valuations. As a result, you'll need to jointly instruct an independent financial specialist to do this and agree as to the most appropriate valuation method. In most cases valuation experts will do a variety of calculations and leave you to choose which one to use, which could be problematic as you may have competing agendas.

Ultimately, lawyers will spend a huge amount of your money arguing over these methods and how to attribute pre-marital value (i.e. what value a business had before you married versus how much of the business's value was generated during the marriage). So, without wanting to sound like a broken record, it comes down to trying to be amicable and seeking a fair compromise rather than pursuing a solo agenda.

Troubleshooting
Failure to disclose all assets is one of the most common reasons why a divorce can be delayed and contested. *amicable* has a 95 per cent success rate, but of the 5 per cent of couples who don't achieve an agreement, the most common reason is a failure to disclose – or that one person believes this is the case.

It's a legal requirement to disclose your assets in full. Non-disclosure is not only legally and morally wrong, it's also counterproductive as, if discovered, it can lead to harsher financial settlements, extra costs, and even criminal proceedings. Ultimately it leaves you without the peace of mind that the finances are 'done' and put to bed ... which is the whole point of doing this formally and having a consent order!

I'm often concerned by the number of people that believe a solicitor or a court has a magic way of 'forcing' their ex to disclose assets, which then might result in lengthy and prohibitively expensive legal and court proceedings in a bid to chase down missing assets. In practice, it is difficult and expensive to prove that someone has hidden assets, and, to do it, you need a forensic accountant and deep, deep pockets beyond most people's means.

So again I return to the point of this book: that being amicable is not just the right thing to do, it's the most cost-effective thing to do even if your ex is not easy to deal with and shady with their assets. Of course, in an ideal world the moral right would win out and bad people would get their comeuppance. But in the real world, good people go bankrupt and lose everything pursing these kinds of scenarios. So my advice is, think carefully before starting down this path – there may be other ways of getting 'enough' of what you want that don't mean gifting your lawyer a new car or holiday of a lifetime!

O is for OPTIONS

Once you know what resources you have, you can start to figure out how to split them to meet your goals. This is more of a problem-solving stage in which you and your partner assess various possible options. You're not approaching this as a lawyer might – 'I am entitled to this and this is my position' – but rather you're going to listen to each other, consider what you could do, and work towards a resolution.

Here a financial/divorce expert is invaluable as they bring a wealth of experience and can discuss your ideas, ask questions and spot any potential problems or imbalances with options. They can also suggest alternative ideas and options that might suit your individual circumstances.

Let's look at the sorts of things you'll need to consider (the options) when it comes to the family home and pensions.

Family home

Determining what happens to the home in a divorce involves complex considerations, including the financial and housing needs of each person, contributions to the property, welfare of any children and overall financial circumstances.

The first step is to talk openly about your living arrangements during and after the divorce. Will one of you stay in the home, or will it be sold and the equity divided? (Equity simply means the value of the property after the mortgage and selling costs are taken into account.) If you have children, their needs should guide these conversations as you'll need to factor in school runs and travel time so they don't spend hours travelling back and forth between homes.

It's also important to be realistic about what you can afford to buy or rent, and to have a backup plan if your first choice isn't possible. Don't forget when considering your options to account for selling costs, potential stamp duty or capital gains tax, and any implications of transferring ownership. Having these details to hand will make discussions clearer and help you to make informed decisions about how best to move forward. You will need professional support to complete any sales or transfers, which might include a conveyancing solicitor, a mortgage advisor, an estate agent or a tax specialist.

It's also worth remembering that the family home holds both monetary and sentimental value, so separating couples may find it difficult to divide it fairly. Common options include:

- Selling it
- One partner buying the other out
- Getting a Mesher order
- Offsetting the value against another asset, such as savings or investments
- Renting it out

What's a Mesher order?

A Mesher order forms part of your consent (financial) order and allows you to postpone the sale of the family home until a particular milestone event, usually when your children have completed their primary or secondary education (sometimes extended to cover their university education).

Crucially, it sorts out what will happen to the proceeds of sale when the property is eventually sold and allows one parent to remain living in the property with the children (without the other parent having rights of entry).

The property remains in joint names throughout and typically you have a clause setting out who is responsible for running costs, and how structural repairs will be dealt with.

Mesher orders aren't necessarily the best option, however. Usually, they are only used if other options such as selling the home and repurchasing are not possible. For example, perhaps there is not enough equity in your property to sell it and buy or create deposits for two separate homes.

The court prefers to have things sorted out at the time of the divorce if achievable, and Mesher orders have

> been criticised for storing up future problems, such as what happens if you still cannot house yourself and adult children in years to come.

Options for dividing a pension

One of the most common mistakes I see being made when people are trying to be amicable over their finances concerns the treatment of pensions. There is a general cultural belief (not helped by the term 'personal pension') that pensions are individual assets that one person has worked hard for and therefore the 'fair' thing to do is let each person keep their own pension. This is misguided and often a big mistake. Here's why:

If, because of the marriage, you have taken on a homemaker role and stayed at home to look after children or taken part-time or lower-paid work to support your partner's career, your pension may be a lot less than your partner's. Perhaps it was decided you couldn't both work sixty-hour weeks, or one of you tended always to pick up the slack if a child was off school. Even if, after the divorce, you go back to work or take on more hours you will have 'lost' the ability to build up your pension in the way your ex has. This needs to be considered and factored into your financial settlement – otherwise you could find yourself being in a completely impoverished position in later life.

Pensions are complex assets. Even if you decide to instruct a divorce solicitor, they won't be a pensions expert, and they cannot provide you with financial advice. So having a bit of basic knowledge means you can then decide what kind of help you need to make sure you don't end up losing out.

There are three main ways to share pensions in a divorce:

- **A pension sharing order** – one partner's pension plan(s) is divided between you when your divorce is finalised. A pension sharing order transfers out a percentage of a pension and pays it to the ex-partner. The recipient will be given a pension credit, not cash, which can be invested in the same pension scheme as their ex or in another external scheme. It's done immediately once the divorce is finalised, not at retirement. There are two ways of calculating pension sharing – you can base it on the CETV, or a more accurate way of dividing a pension is to have an actuarial report and calculate how to divide the pensions to ensure equal income in retirement.
- **Offsetting** – one partner keeps their more valuable pension plan(s) in exchange for taking less of the other capital assets; for example, they take less of the equity in the family home or your combined savings. This is the most common way people handle pensions – but

not always the best! A cash pound and pension pound may have different values so you may be comparing apples and pears.
- **A pension attachment order** – the court can order a pension provider to pay a percentage of the income from one person's pension on divorce to the partner. This can also be or include a pension commutable lump sum and/or death benefits to an ex-spouse once the pension is in payment. Pension attachment orders are rarely used now as they keep former spouses financially tied together; a clean break is seen as preferable. In addition, if there is a pension attachment order and the pension holder dies before retiring, their ex-spouse may receive nothing.

Of course, you may have other assets that need to be considered, so what are the more general principles of keeping things amicable when dividing assets?

- Keep an open mind – approach discussions as problem-solving rather than a win/lose situation.
- Be willing to compromise – recognise that you may not get everything you want, but aim for a fair balance. It's only a solution if you both get enough of what you want.
- Use constructive language – ask questions like 'What might work for both of us?' instead of stating fixed positions.

- Focus on needs, not wants – think about what you and any children need to move forward securely.
- Be transparent – share financial information openly to build trust and reduce conflict.
- Stay future-focused – concentrate on workable solutions that set you both up for the next stage of life.
- Listen actively – give each other space to explain your priorities without interruption.

W is for WAY FORWARD

You need to decide which are the best options for you and which ones achieve your goals both now and in the future. Before deciding, you could engage a financial advisor to do some cash-flow modelling to show the kind of income you might expect to have from a pension or investments throughout your life. It may also be that your finances are far less complex – perhaps you have just a house and joint bank account to split – so you have fewer options.

Once you have agreed on how to divide your finances, you can move ahead with drawing up a consent order. At *amicable* we document everything into a Record of Agreement Form (RAF) in which we outline, in plain and accessible English, what has been agreed for couples to review. Once they're happy we then draft the consent order, and for this you need a legal professional to ensure it is drafted correctly so that the court will approve it and make it legally binding.

By reaching this stage, you've worked through and agreed the finances with your partner, which will give you both a sense of ownership. You've had a voice, thought through the options, and built the foundation for the next stage of your life.

> ### Case study: A tailored agreement
> *A couple came to one of our divorce specialists looking for help to agree a financial agreement, which one of them had been advised he should not accept. They were both really happy with their agreement because it was in line with things they had discussed and agreed from the outset of their relationship and they were frustrated that traditional legal services were forcing them into a prolonged battle. They were being grown-up, were fully informed and understood what the relationship had given them.*
>
> I worked with a couple who'd got together ten years before and there was quite a big age difference between them. The younger partner was French, the older was British. They had a nice house in central London and lots of assets were brought into the marriage. Within a couple of years, their marriage had effectively ended but they continued living together as friends and supporting each other. This had worked well for a while until the younger partner decided she wanted to return to France. To get her on her feet, the older husband bought her a property and helped her start a business in France.

When it came to their divorce, they had decided to go for roughly a 90/10 split of assets (in favour of the older husband). When he came to me, he said, 'Look, we're both really happy with this but I'm being told there's no way the split will go through the courts.'

I explained that we could help but we would need to speak to both of them and work as a couple. We could do this without getting separate lawyers who would put something together that on paper the court might sign off but which wouldn't meet their needs and would leave them feeling bitter. Instead, we would draft an order and put in a lengthy explanation to the court explaining their thinking and honouring their agreement.

They decided not to use lawyers, I took them through the process, and we got it through the court. The judge did ask to speak to them both, but once it was clear they were equally happy and no one was taking advantage of anyone, the judge approved the consent order.

In summary

- Talking about money and making decisions about how to divide it fairly can be challenging. Acknowledge that you and your partner might have a different relationship with money.
- Try not to dwell on what has happened in the past and focus on your needs now and in the future. This is a good time to redefine your relationship with money on your own terms.
- Think about what you want your life to look like after divorce. Work out what is important to you and focus on these goals.
- Take into consideration what is important to your partner, be open to looking at various options, and try to be flexible ... it's only a 'deal' if you are both content.
- If you feel like you've made fair and reasonable decisions over the finances, you'll feel more in control and set up for the future and you will learn a lot.

9

From Us to Me: Life After Love

What happens when the final order arrives and you are now, after months of paperwork, finally divorced? Will you collapse into a heap of tears or jump around with joy? Or will the news, quietly dropping into your inbox with little fanfare, feel strangely anticlimactic? It's hard to predict how you'll feel but I certainly remember feeling completely underwhelmed when my divorce finally came through, while feeling totally overwhelmed by what had gone before and what lay ahead.

It marks a profound shift, the transition from 'us' to 'me', which can be disorientating, and, as I found, incredibly lonely. Weekends, when other 'intact' families were spending time together, were the hardest. It was the stark realisation that I would be putting the bins out *every* week and making every single cup of tea or meal. It's talking to the TV, and realising that not seeing your kids every day is the toughest thing you'll ever face.

And yet, while it might not seem it, separation or divorce really does give you an opportunity to re-evaluate your life, to close one chapter and open a new one, and to move forward – maybe not right now but at some point – with positivity. Divorcing amicably doesn't necessarily take away the pain, but it can ease the path forward. When respect is maintained, it's easier to co-parent, communicate and rebuild your life with less resentment weighing you down and, most importantly, if you've got kids, you still feel like a family – just one that lives in different homes.

This chapter will help you to navigate life after divorce, first by exploring the mixed emotions you may feel when the final order drops and then with tips on how to heal and recover in the period afterwards. I will also give practical guidance on building financial stability after divorce, on successful co-parenting, introducing new partners and ways to create a happy future for you and your family.

The final order

The divorce process involves lots of waiting around for various bits of paperwork to transit through the courts – you've been through the twenty-week cooling-off period, filled in a ton of forms, and waited at least six weeks after receiving the conditional order. Then, six, eight, twelve months later, you finally press the button to apply for the final order, and – whoosh! – there it is in your inbox sometimes only twenty-four hours later.

After the endless back and forth, the trawling through finances, the seesawing of emotions, the moment that ends a major chapter of your life comes not with a bang but the underwhelming ping of an email. It informs you that your final order has been granted, meaning your divorce is legally binding and final, and is sent as a PDF which you can download. It's a legal document, so keep it safe (either by saving or printing it) as you'll need it for financial matters, such as any pensions sharing you may have in your consent order, or if you remarry or change your name. It takes the form of a single piece of A4 paper, more akin to a formal letter than a certificate, with details of your court case, relevant names, dates and electronic court seal or crest.

When I divorced for the second time, in 2012, it was still the practice to receive an actual piece of paper – a proper document with an official red stamp on it. It felt quite tactile and formal and fitting for such an important milestone. It's not quite the same with an automated email. The whole online process certainly streamlines the divorce process and I'm a big fan of tech but what we've gained in ease we've lost in ceremony or solemnification of certain events.

Of course, you might feel differently to me when you receive yours – perhaps you'll feel triumphant when you thought you'd feel sad, or strangely empty and more than happy to close your laptop and get on with your day. The point is it's hard to know how you'll feel once it's over and it might not be what you or your friends were expecting. For that reason, you need to create some space for yourself so you can sit with your feelings. Life doesn't stop when the final order comes through – you might be co-parenting, setting up a new house and as busy as ever – but if you can, try to take a breath and acknowledge what's just happened.

If you decide you want to mark the divorce, perhaps with something more than a piece of paper that looks like a parking fine, you could create your own ending or ceremony. It can be something very low-key or something more extravagant – whatever will help you to gain some closure, create space for something new or even just to celebrate your resilience over the past few months. Here are some ideas:

- Have a day or a weekend away to reflect
- Print out the final order, hold it in your hands, read it aloud and follow with a toast (then file it and keep it safely!)
- Write down how you feel or write some vows to yourself about what you want going forward
- Light a candle or a lantern or let off some fireworks
- Plant some seeds, trees or a flower/herb garden to mark the next chapter of your life
- Buy yourself a present – jewellery, new speakers or headphones, or even a tattoo
- Go watch your favourite band or sports team – live, or at a mate's house
- Mark the occasion with some friends, perhaps a dinner or divorce party, complete with divorce cake

- Do something practical – there's plenty of important admin left to do – which will help you take control of your life and move on

After my divorce, I took a bit of time off work – I didn't have much money, but I was willing to cut corners and badly needed some time to decompress and unravel from the whole process. I had moved into a new house, and I threw myself into doing it up and creating a home for me and my kids. I went out shopping with friends, trawling through salvage yards and second-hand shops for bits and pieces for the house. I could choose exactly what I wanted, without having to agree it with anyone else or make compromises, and that felt very freeing and healing.

In those early days/weeks/months, treat yourself with compassion. Keeping up with the basic maintenance of life – eating well, exercise and sleep – makes a good foundation for recovery. In that period, I had trouble quietening my mind and getting off to sleep, and I had to learn how to switch off all the thoughts whirling through my mind – methods that still serve me well today.

You might choose to see a counsellor or therapist to process some of what you're feeling, although, as with bereavement or grief, you don't want to do this too soon and disrupt the normal process of healing. You need to try to pick a time after you've processed some of the very raw feelings, before you then do any deeper work.

Ultimately – and this may come further down the line – you want to make sense of the divorce; you want to learn from it, come away knowing something about yourself that will give you skills for the future, and to make you feel like there was a point to it.

Other tips for healing post-divorce

Divorce often means a change in day-to-day life, which can feel unsettling at first. Creating new routines can help bring a sense of comfort and structure to your days.

- It might be something simple like a weekend walk, trying new recipes or joining a regular class or group. These routines help to shape your life and give you something to look forward to. Even simple mindfulness activities can help bring new moments of joy to support your healing journey.
- If you have children, starting new family traditions together can help everyone adjust. Whether it's pancake mornings, a monthly movie evening, or – let's be realistic – funniest meme on TikTok night, small rituals can create warmth and connection in your new family dynamic, allowing you to make new and positive memories together.
- Having something to work towards, even something small, can bring you a sense of purpose and direction

when things feel uncertain. These goals could be as simple as learning a new skill, improving your fitness or planning a trip you've always wanted to take.
- You may have had shared interests with your ex-partner that no longer feel special anymore, or perhaps you have more time on your hands now, and want to put it to good use. Lots of us have passions and interests that we've never had time to follow before – and now is as good a time as any to give them a try!
- Try to identify small positives in your daily life. This could be as simple as a good conversation with a friend, a peaceful moment to yourself, or progress you've made in adjusting to your new circumstances.
- Gratitude doesn't mean pretending everything is perfect or ignoring the challenges. Instead, it helps balance difficult emotions by highlighting the good things still present in your life.

Identity and purpose

When my divorce was going through, I felt my whole life revolved around the process – my thoughts, actions and energy were all funnelled into the various agreements and decisions I had to make. Once the divorce was over, it took me some time to redefine my identity, purpose and meaning in life. I didn't work directly before the divorce and quite a bit of my identity was tied to family and being a stay-at-home mum and running our family house, which we were in the process of building.

After the divorce, I had to adjust and find a new identity as a single parent and a working mum. My ex moved away so I had sole care of our children, but if you and your ex are now co-parenting and running two households, what are you when you're not with your children or partner? If you've always worked, and your identity was all about your work, how are you going to integrate your role as a more hands-on parent to your children?

Divorce marks a transition, from 'us' back to 'you', giving you a chance to reconnect to the person you were before your relationship. Think about what you loved doing before your marriage, revisit some of those hobbies, reconnect with some old friends or make new ones who can support your growth, and find new hobbies that speak to the person you have grown into. It may be that you need to find work or get a different job, and this too can help you to redefine yourself and do things on your own terms.

At the same time, don't let divorce define you – try not to make it the first thing you mention when meeting someone new. You are more than your divorce, so don't let it become your whole story and instead focus on what comes next. As part of reclaiming your identity, you might choose to change your name (see below), take control of your finances – perhaps for the first time in your life – and start afresh.

> I don't need to forgive my ex, only to move on and focus on the future ... It's good to sit in the sad, to be angry, to process it. But then it comes to a point, and, well, how do I want to use my energy? Always hateful towards a person, or being positive about a new life I've been given?
> *Helen Thorne, author and podcaster*

The practical stuff

Be prepared: there is quite a lot of personal admin to do once you are officially divorced, and only by doing this will you fully untangle your legal, financial and personal ties. In fact, you could say the final order marks the end of a marathon, but as you cross the finish line you discover you have to climb a staircase to get your medal! You've done the hard, exhausting part but there's still the necessary and sometimes frustrating paperwork to get done before it's complete.

Here's a checklist of what you should be sorting post-divorce – some essential, others optional.

1. Organise important documents relating to the divorce, keeping both digital and printed copies in a safe place. These include: the final order, conditional order, financial consent order (including the pensions sharing annex where appropriate) and parenting plan.

2. Update records. If you're changing your name, you need to update it on various documents; on some of these you also need to amend your marital status. You should aim to do this within a month of receiving your final order. These include:

- Passport
- Driving licence
- National Insurance record (marital status)
- Bank accounts
- Credit/store cards
- Medical records
- Tax and HMRC records
- Insurance policies
- Utilities
- Council tax
- Electoral register
- Work-related records
- Pension schemes

Divorced or single?

When updating your marital status on official records, you should tick 'divorced' not 'single'. This applies to all legal and financial documents, pensions and insurance policies, employment and HR records. Technically 'single' means you've never legally been married, whereas being divorced means you once were but are no longer legally married, and the distinction can affect legal rights, financial assessments, visa and immigration applications among other things. (Personally, I wish there was a NOYFB box!) In more informal settings, with friends, dates and the like, you can of course call yourself 'single'.

When it comes to titles, Ms is commonly chosen by divorced or separated women, but you can still be a Mrs or Miss or Mx – it's a personal preference and not a rule and if you are only changing your prefix you do not need to change using a deed poll.

3. Check if you're entitled to benefits or tax relief. If you have informed HMRC of your new marital status, your tax code may change and you may be entitled to tax relief. Also, you could check with the Department for Work and Pensions to see if you are eligible for benefits or inform them if you already receive benefits. Council tax reductions may apply if you live on your own. The charity Turn2us can provide further information on whether you can claim any benefits (see **turn2us.org.uk**).

Note that child benefit can only be claimed by one parent so you need to decide who that will be.

4. Sort your finances. Ideally, if you've been following the *amicable* divorce advice you will have sorted your consent order out before applying for your final order – but if you haven't, you should arrange to sort this as soon as possible. You'll need a legal professional to help you draft this.

5. Close joint bank accounts and investments if you're not keeping one for co-parenting. After your divorce your financial situation will probably look very different. Now that you're flying solo, you need to get a good grasp of your finances (whether or not you were the 'money person' in your previous relationship). Take another look at your income, available funds and outgoings and assess whether you need to retune your lifestyle or redefine some of your expectations. Make a budget that reflects your new reality and, if you can, save money for an emergency fund, just so you have a buffer for any unforeseen events.

    Now is a great time to get some financial advice, such as a money coach at Octopus Money. It may be that you need to set up a pension or assess your current pension to see if your current contributions will get you to where you want to be by retirement. A money coach can help you to create a plan, manage expenses and debt, save for the future and create wealth.

6. Update legal documents. Update your will ASAP – a divorce doesn't invalidate your will but you may need to change beneficiaries, executors or any trustees. Also

you may need to update any power of attorneys, life insurance policies or trusts. Check your consent order because sometimes people make undertakings in their orders to write something in or out of their will and there is usually a timescale attached.

7. Check security, emergency contacts and subscriptions. Change passwords and check shared devices and accounts and remove access if needed. Inform schools and GP of new status and set up new emergency contacts.

8. Cancel or transfer any joint subscriptions or memberships. This book is all about taking an amicable route so one tip I would give you here is to make sure you communicate with your ex if you are changing things that affect them. I remember being in a complete panic when I realised my ex used to insure the cars and he hadn't told me when the renewal date was! Be kind – let each other know so things don't create hassle for the other person.

Should I change my name?

Changing your name can be a powerful way to mark a new chapter in life, especially if you feel a strong need to let go of ties to your past relationship. Women may decide to revert to their maiden name if they changed it when they got married, and men are also entitled to reassume a birth surname if they had taken their partner's name. Both men and women might want to remove part of a double-barrelled surname if they had one during marriage. Similarly, you might even decide to start your new life with a completely new surname. To do this or to change double-barrelled surnames, you'll need to obtain a deed poll.

You do not need to obtain a deed poll if you are reverting to your maiden or birth name. A final order is usually accepted by government bodies and companies, although some organisations (such as HM Passport Office) might require a marriage certificate or birth certificate.

Once you have the relevant documents you need to start notifying companies and government bodies. On average a name changer notifies approximately twenty-four different organisations. Companies like NameSwitch (**nameswitch.co.uk**) can help you with the process.

You can change your name whenever you want – there's no legal timeframe here. But note that there are ramifications if you have a different surname to your children. Be aware also that you can't change your children's surnames without the permission of their other parent (assuming they have parental responsibility).

If you travel abroad with your children and you have different names on your passports you can be questioned on this (irrespective of whether you have a letter of consent from your ex). In some countries, you need to carry documentation to say that you can travel alone with your children if both parents aren't with them. When travelling to South Africa, for example, you need to have a notarised document if you're travelling alone with children.

Your children also might have strong views on the issue of names. When I divorced, my kids were adamant they wanted us all to have the same name, so I decided to keep it. There is the option to double-barrel your name, with both your married and maiden name, although there still may be complications when you travel abroad with your children.

Wedding and engagement rings

In ticking off those administrative tasks, you might also be wondering what to do with your wedding or engagement rings if you have them. I sold my engagement ring to refurbish my house, and for me this felt like the right thing to do. I wanted to invest in my new home, and new life, and I wasn't in a financial position to repurpose the diamond for another piece of jewellery.

Of course, there's no rush to do anything with your rings – you could put them in a drawer forever, or until you decide what to do with them. If you decide you want to do something practical with them, here are a few ideas:

- **Sell them** – you might want to clear out anything to do with your marriage or need to generate as much cash as you can to support yourself after divorce. You could use the money to buy a different piece of jewellery or something that simply makes you happy. Alternatively, you could donate the money to a charity or a good cause so that someone profits from your life step. Bear in mind, however, that resale values are much lower than if you were to buy new and you'll be lucky to get back 50 per cent of what you paid for the jewellery in the first place.

- **Redesign them** – sometimes it feels like too big a step to get rid of your jewellery, even if you won't wear it anymore. Speak to a jeweller about having the rings reworked, perhaps into a different type of ring, a 'right-hand' ring or an entirely different piece. One of my clients had the three stones in her engagement ring changed to make a pendant and a pair of earrings, which she plans to hand to her children when they are older.
- **Pass them on** – you could keep them and pass them on to future generations. Your marriage or love may not have lasted but they may still have emotional value to your children, for instance. You could also donate your rings to a charity.

Dating

The thought of dating and finding a new partner might be way down your to-do list after divorce. Perhaps you're enjoying being on your own, watching whatever you want on TV, and the whole swiping left or right or creating the perfect profile (with or without your dog?) feels like a world you don't want to enter right now.

On the flip side, you might be super keen to date: maybe you've already downloaded five dating apps and are hitting the gym in preparation. Men are a little more likely to fall into this camp – some figures suggest 64 per cent of men will remarry after divorce compared to 52 per cent of women. Another survey of 2,000 adults, from the US in 2012, found 47 per cent of divorced men were eager to remarry compared to just 20 per cent of divorced women. It may be that men miss the emotional support of a partner more keenly, whereas women traditionally rely on friends more and these days are less financially reliant on men.

Do whatever helps you to move on and be happy, but be careful about dating before you're ready. It's probably best not to embark on a serious relationship if you're feeling mentally fragile or are in a panicked state of 'I can't be on my own!' This was me after my first divorce and I spent months in therapy practising being on my own – everything from deliberately not making plans on a Friday night (which nearly broke me!) to eating in a restaurant alone (in the days pre-smartphones!) to going on a mini-break on your own. I won't lie, it was tough, but it was probably the best money I ever spent and set me up for a much freer life.

Before you date, it's a good idea to wait until you are comfortable in your skin, have learned to be on your own a little, know what you want and are mentally ready to share your life with someone (if that's what you're after). Relationship expert Rachael Lloyd explained to me on a recent podcast what can happen if you date when you're not ready:

> 'If you are rushing, ask yourself, what's the evidence that I'm ready? And what's the evidence that I may not be ready?
>
> Because it could be that you just want to fix those challenging feelings you've been having if you're in a hurry. And when you do that, it can work, but the risk is that you'll either get into things quickly and find that you bail, or you'll be making ill-informed choices, just looking for that sort of comfort. Because dating for some people is a kind of painkiller and a cushion against where they are in their life.
>
> So I would recommend gently easing in – that would be my advice.'

Once you are ready to meet new people, where do you start? There are of course plenty of tools out there to help you, including dating apps, websites and dating agencies. The dating apps – Bumble, Hinge, Tinder, etc. – are great for people comfortable with tech and who are happy to browse through lots of profiles. Websites like eHarmony or high-end dating agencies filter out matches for you based on your preferences, although costs or fees are higher.

Somewhere in between online dating and an exclusive dating agency is something I have personally experienced – a dating coach! If you've listened to *The Divorce Podcast*, you may remember James Preece, a dating coach who gave us lots of tips about getting back on the dating horse, and after our conversation I contacted him and asked for his help. Again, money well spent, as it gave me the confidence to get back out there, to know what I wanted and how to stay safe, weed out time wasters and stop being so picky. He helped me with advice on dating apps, choosing people, profile writing, first-date etiquette, and even introduced me to speed dating – which was honestly the best fun ever (and thank you Lisa for coming with me!). Like house hunting, you have to 'see' properties yourself to know whether you want them!

You can of course go old school and meet people by getting out and about. Trying new hobbies (which is also great for your recovery) – whether it's a running club, walking group, book club, dinner-party group or whatever – is a good way to meet like-minded people. As dating coach James said:

> The very act of telling the universe you're ready to go out there and do something can definitely start to make the magic happen. Sitting around at home, waiting for someone to knock on your door, just won't work! So get yourself out there in some way or another, and dating apps and dating sites can be

really good if you know what you're doing, if you have good pictures, a good profile, and you're proactive.

Here are a few extra tips when it comes to dating:

You won't know unless you try

It's very common to feel nervous about dating. It may have been a long time since you last dated and it's difficult to know how you'll feel about it until you try. You can always just dip your toe in the water – you don't need to go 'full throttle', five dates a week! As relationship expert Rachael Lloyd advises, take your time, see it as an adventure and an opportunity to get to know people. Every experience, even the bad dates, you'll have a takeaway, you'll have learned something new.

Safety first

If you're meeting someone for the first time, or you've met them through an app or social media platform, remember to meet in a public place and tell a friend or loved one where you are. It might be nerve-wracking to tell a friend that you're going on a date, especially if they knew your ex-partner. But your personal safety is the most important thing.

If you feel unsafe or uncomfortable at any point, leave. Tell your friend when you're home and this can also be a good opportunity to debrief after the date. It's easy to think this applies just to women – it doesn't. Safety is everyone's priority.

Don't compare your dates with your ex

Think about what you want from an encounter – companionship, sex, a relationship or just to see where it goes. If you are looking for something more serious or long term, try to analyse what wasn't so positive about your last relationship and how you can avoid this. Be aware of the old pendulum swing and try not to go to the extreme opposite of your ex – it seldom works. It's not a good idea, however, to compare everyone you date with your ex, and while it's useful to learn from your previous relationship, being overly critical can lead to no one quite fitting the bill. After all, everyone is unique, so trying to shoehorn a new person into your ex's shoes will likely lead to disappointment.

> **Case study: Paul**
>
> *Integrative therapist Paul Huntingford experienced a traumatic end to his three-year marriage, with punishing divorce proceedings that took two years to go through. Things went sour after the involvement of solicitors, ultimately leading to a complete breakdown in communication between Paul and his ex. The experience impacted Paul's mental health and after the divorce he retrained as a therapist. Here he talks about life after divorce, including early mistakes with dating, and how much his life has changed.*

The breakdown of a relationship doesn't have to be about a failure. It can be about the kind of joys that you've had and how you've grown together. And in fact, as difficult as my marriage was, I have definitely learned from it.

It was incredibly painful at the time, but over the years I've managed to see, okay, how has that made me grow as a person? And in terms of my personal relationships now, they're very different to how they were before I was in that relationship.

I was actually very relieved to get out of the marriage. And then I quite quickly got into another relationship, probably about four months after having a break. And within three months, I was kind of fast-forwarded into a very similar dynamic that was going on in my marriage. And it was scary, very scary. I only then decided, right, I've really got to concentrate on what I'm actually doing and to work through whatever is going on so I can change what I'm doing.

It's the kind of Freudian repetition compulsion of doing the same thing that we're just programmed to do, because we have a set way of being in relationships. I think that that's really important because you can't control the other person, whether it's your ex or the new mister or missus, whoever you're going to meet. You have no control over that. What you do have control over is insight into yourself, your behaviours, the things that are likely to trigger you, the traps you're likely to fall into.

Divorce definitely changed my life, it's changed my career, it's changed how I am in relationships with other people, changed what I do socially, absolutely everything really. And that has been a good thing. But I also see how it can be very difficult, how it can be a very lonely time. And it's not easy to find support systems out there sometimes, and it can feel like life has fallen apart in some way, and rebuilding it can seem very scary. And it takes a lot of courage to sometimes pick up the pieces and keep going.

Dating and children

Dating if you have children adds an extra layer of complexity as it's not just about your own feelings and needs but also theirs. There's the practical issue of finding a babysitter if your children are young or fitting a date into your shared-care arrangement and busy life.

How much you tell your children depends on their age. Being open and honest with your children is important but there should be a clear difference between how you talk to them versus how you talk to one of your friends. If you feel it's appropriate to talk to them about the fact you're dating, don't over-share; tell them only what you feel they should know and give them an opportunity to digest the news and ask any questions.

When you feel it's time to introduce a new partner to your children, do so slowly and carefully. Remember you may have decided that you're ready to move on but that doesn't mean that the children are. If you worked up a parenting plan with your ex, you may have already agreed how best to introduce new partners. Whether it's you or your ex introducing a new partner, it's best if you first discuss it with each other so everyone knows what's happening.

When you do tell them, reassure them that you're not trying to replace the other parent, that nothing's going to happen quickly, the circumstances aren't suddenly going to dramatically change overnight, and you just want to make sure everyone is happy. Just do things slowly and remember you're all at different stages of this journey.

Your ex and new partners

Learning that your ex has met someone new can be deeply unsettling and might trigger a variety of emotions. Knowing that they then might be introduced to your children can make the whole process even more painful. As parents, you don't have the right to stop each other introducing your children to new partners but it can be a tricky path to negotiate. The ideal scenario is if you can meet your ex's new partner first, just so you can have an introductory chat and perhaps allay some of your fears – after all, they will be spending time with your children so it's natural to want to know a bit about them. You obviously need to be reassured they won't be a risk to your children, that they will be kind and your children will feel secure. The more you can communicate with any new partners, the better, but I appreciate how tough this can be.

Dealing with the feelings that come up when you know your children are part of 'another family' with your ex and their new partner is hard. Jealousy, bitterness, feelings of loss, concern for their welfare and even FOMO are all common, normal and something that as single parents we have to get our heads round. There is a big difference between genuine concern (a new partner presents a real risk) and not knowing who the new partner is.

When your children have met a new partner, don't be tempted to question them. Remember they're adapting to a new life also and might be finding the whole process unsettling. Your job is to provide calm, steady reassurance and let them know it's okay to have a mix of emotions and they can talk to you about anything. Try to keep your own emotions separate from theirs.

Blended families

At some point (if it hasn't happened already), you or your ex may begin a serious relationship or start living with someone who has children – or who will be living with yours. In these situations, a blended family is formed, which may include step-parents, step-siblings and half-siblings.

It's by no means an unusual set-up – in the UK it's estimated that at least 10 per cent of children live with a step-parent (although the data on this is not exact and figures are likely to be higher). In the US, approximately 16 per cent of children live in blended families.

Adjusting to the new dynamics of a blended family can be challenging, especially when there's a conflict of loyalty and different parenting styles. But if you persevere and continue to communicate effectively with your ex, they can bring joy, love and connection and long-term rewards. Here are a few tips on how best to navigate them.

Take time to get to know one another

It's only natural to want to progress things quickly but it's important to take your time once children are involved. All blended families have experienced some form of loss, either through a divorce, separation or the death of a partner/parent.

Everyone grieves differently, so while you and your partner are ready to move on, the children, other biological partners, grandparents or even friends might be finding it difficult to adjust. It generally takes several years for a blended family to integrate.

Take time to get to know everyone, and for them to get to know you. Spend time together having fun and making memories. When we're happy we're more likely to be ourselves and can relax – just have fun together!

Work out what role you want in the family

This might sound obvious, but in reality the role of stepmum or stepdad is very vague. You could be a 'replacement' parent at one end of the scale, especially if their biological parent is no longer around, or at the other, you could be more of a friend to your partner's children, particularly if they are older and you only see them from time to time. The most important thing is to agree on your role with your partner and check you have the same expectations. There are no fixed rules; it's just important you and your partner keep talking and work out what you're both comfortable with and what works in your family.

It's about enhancement not replacement

When a blended family first emerges, it is pretty likely that there will be animosity, trust issues, guardedness and wanting to keep your child with you, rather than sharing them with a 'new' mother or father. But remember: the stepparent is pretty unlikely to replace the biological parent in terms of how they are seen by the child. This doesn't mean that the child can't develop a rich, loving, meaningful relationship with them that sits wonderfully alongside the biological parent. But it does mean you can stop feeling put out and jealous. If you can realise that your child will benefit and thrive from these new relationships, then this will help shift your mindset to become more accepting, thereby creating a less acrimonious environment for your child.

Take your lead from the children and think about the language you'll use

It can be hard but it's important to try and take things at a pace children in the family are happy with. Children want to be loyal to their biological parents so it's often hard for them to work out how to deal with step-parents. Try and let them know that they can choose how to refer to you. Children like to blend in so they may refer to step-parents as Mum or Dad when they're in public but use their first names in private. Just let them know that just because they call you Mum or Dad doesn't mean that you are in any way replacing their biological mum or dad.

Setting rules and boundaries in a blended family can be tricky

Work out key messages that you tell your child so they hear the same things from significant people in their lives. If you can, set similar rules around bedtimes, screen time, mealtimes and responses to certain behaviours.

The general advice is for the biological parent to take charge of discipline in the early days. Children are going to resist listening to a step-parent at the beginning of a relationship and will always defer to their biological parents. However, as time moves on, particularly once you live together (even some of the time), it's important that as a step-parent you feel you have a voice and are listened to! It's best to have a few clear house 'rules' or 'boundaries'. This can be as simple as taking shoes off, putting plates in the dishwasher or tidying their room. It's important that the step-parent feels they have some authority in their own home and, importantly, have the support of their partner. The children need to feel that you are both in charge and need to listen to both of you.

Remember who you're doing this for

When we aim to make a blended family work, we do it for the sake of our children, so they can have clear, amicable access to both of their parents and their new partners without picking up on any negativity. Stepping into their shoes to remember that can be very helpful for us when we feel angry or jealous that our children aren't with us all the time.

Ultimately, you want your children to feel loved and the more people who can love your children the better. Things are different now, you're co-parenting in a different way – there may be teething problems and bumps along the way – but if you can get it right, you and your children will benefit hugely.

Case study: Silver linings

I love this story from one of our divorce specialists, who chose to share it in our group Teams chat recently. Her separation was a real shock to her and she and her partner genuinely had a really rocky start to their co-parenting.

I wanted to share something that really stayed with me recently. I was driving with my daughter Sophie last week, and we were chatting about memories from when she was younger and I was still with her dad. At some point, I asked her if she ever wished we were still together. Without hesitation, she looked at me and said, 'No! I wouldn't have Greg [my partner] and Sarah [her dad's partner] in my life if you guys were still together!'

Her answer really made me think. It wasn't just the speed of her response, but the certainty in her voice. In that moment, I realised how differently children can see things – how they can focus on the good that has come from change, even when that change was difficult.

For me, separation had been full of challenges and emotional ups and downs, and there were moments when I questioned whether I'd done the right thing. But hearing Sophie's perspective reminded me that separation isn't only about what's lost – it's also about what's gained.

New friendships, blended families and opportunities to grow can emerge in ways you never expected.

> That one conversation was a powerful reminder that sometimes our children see the silver linings before we do, and that moving forward can lead to happiness we couldn't have imagined at the time. Looking back now, I honestly wouldn't change a thing!

In summary

- When your divorce finally comes through, you may have mixed emotions. Treat yourself with compassion and allow yourself to heal and recover. If you feel ready, you could see a counsellor or therapist.
- Don't forget to deal with all the practical admin after divorce, and make sure you're on top of your finances. If you haven't sorted a financial remedy order, do this straight away.
- Don't rush into dating or meeting someone new until you're mentally ready to share your life again with someone, if that's what you want.
- If you have children, keep their needs as your priority as you move forward and ensure they feel loved and secure.
- Learn from your divorce, reconnect with the person you were before your relationship, and move into the future with positivity. Your new life can come slowly. And breathe!

A Final Note

The life that you have after divorce – whether you're co-parenting with your ex, looking to meet someone new, or are happy to be on your own – can be everything you want it to be.

You now have a chance to recalibrate your life, to pivot in a different direction. Your divorce may have been emotionally challenging, but my hope is you were able to navigate through any hurt or past conflict and separate amicably. By doing so you'll emerge feeling less scathed by the whole process, able to communicate with your ex if you need to, and in a better frame of mind to move on to the next stage of your life.

We should take the bond of marriage or civil partnership seriously but at the same time we need to recognise that relationships falter and that staying in a dysfunctional one causes not just unhappiness but also harm. Divorce or separation doesn't necessarily negatively impact children; it's ongoing conflict or the absence of a parent that can cause problems. Added to that, no one should feel compelled to stay in an abusive or failing marriage just to meet the expectations of family, culture or society.

Divorce or separation should be accessible for everyone, and all involved should be safe and able to secure a financially viable future. We shouldn't be making divorce or separation a punitive or punishing process, in which couples are encouraged to battle it out, to cut off all communication just at a time when what's most needed is respect and kindness.

In so many cases, partners simply grow in different directions – we can't control another person's growth and shouldn't feel shame or guilt when a relationship comes to an end. It's a fact of life – relationships can and do run their course. Perhaps you made the choice, or perhaps you were on the receiving end of someone else's choice and, while you may have had little control over the decision, you can have control over your response, how you separate and what your life will look life afterwards.

I hope I have supported you in some way on the divorce journey and shown how, with good communication, cooperation and mutual respect, you can separate amicably and build a new life with positivity. But, even if your partner is not respectful, unable to communicate or unwilling to cooperate, I hope you have found in this book some ways to wrest back control and do what's right for you.

Divorce can create an opportunity and a jumping-off point for people, and can spark smarter, more empowered

a final note

decisions ahead and the beginning of something meaningful. An amicable divorce or separation means your family isn't broken, but is just evolving and finding a new shape – where each member can grow, heal and continue to thrive.

Resources

A list of agencies and charities offering support for domestic abuse can be found at gov.uk/guidance/domestic-abuse-how-to-get-help

amicable – amicable.co.uk

The *amicable* website provides tools and advice for separating couples and the friends and family supporting them, as well as guidance on choosing the right *amicable* service to suit your situation. Also listed below are links to specific tools to help with your divorce.

amicable agreement checker – check your financial agreement will meet the court's criteria: amicable.co.uk/amicable-agreement-checker

amicable co-parenting app: amicable.co.uk/coparenting-app

amicable space – support community for people navigating divorce: amicable.space

Court fee calculator – check whether you qualify for a court fee discount: amicable.co.uk/divorce-court-fees-calculator

Parenting plan: amicable.co.uk/parenting-plan-ebook

Separating with Children Service: amicable.co.uk/separating-with-children-service

The Divorce Podcast: thedivorcepodcast.com

Join our community

Instagram: @amicable_world

TikTok: @amicable_world

X: @amicable_world

Threads: @amicable_world

Facebook: facebook.com/amicableapps

LinkedIn: linkedin.com/company/amicable-divorce

YouTube: youtube.com/@amicable_world

Rules and guidance for divorces in Scotland or Northern Ireland

Scottish government website: gov.scot

Scottish Court and Tribunals Service: scotcourts.gov.uk/taking-action/divorce-and-dissolution-of-civil-partnership

Northern Ireland government services: nidirect.gov.uk/articles/getting-divorce-or-dissolving-civil-partnership

Government resources

England and Wales divorce proceedings: gov.uk/divorce

Child maintenance calculator: gov.uk/calculate-child-maintenance

Child Maintenance Service: gov.uk/child-maintenance-service

Form D81: gov.uk/government/publications/form-d81-statement-of-information-for-a-consent-order-in-relation-to-a-financial-remedy.

Note that completing the D81 alone is not sufficient information for the court to approve your financial arrangements. You must also send the court a legally drafted document called a consent order or financial order along with the D81.

Form A: gov.uk/government/publications/form-a-notice-of-intention-to-proceed-with-an-application-for-a-financial-order
Use this form to start a request for a financial order in proceedings for divorce or ending a civil partnership.

gov.uk/money-property-when-relationship-ends/get-court-to-decide
A general resource that sets out the process for whether you are in contested or amicable proceedings.

General advice for divorce, separation and parenting

amicable: amicable.co.uk

Cafcass (the Children and Family Court Advisory and Support Service): cafcass.gov.uk

Citizens Advice (gives advice on many areas, including financial entitlements like benefits and tax credits): citizensadvice.org.uk

OnePlusOne: oneplusone.org.uk

OnlyMums & Dads: onlymumsanddads.org

Single parents/parenting

Asian Single Parents Network: aspnetwork.org.uk

Gingerbread: gingerbread.org.uk

Counselling

BetterHelp: betterhelp.com

British Association for Counselling and Psychotherapy – find a therapist: bacp.co.uk

Drug addiction support: nhs.uk/live-well/addiction-support/drug-addiction-getting-help

Gamble Aware: gambleaware.org

Place2Be – children's mental health support: place2be.org.uk

Relate: relate.org.uk

Split Happens – resource for teens whose parents are separating: splithappens.co.uk

Legal advice and legal processes

Advicenow: advicenow.org.uk

Family Mediation Council (FMC): familymediationcouncil.org.uk

Institute of Family Law Arbitrators (IFLA): ifla.org.uk

LawWorks – free legal advice: lawworks.org.uk

Name Switch: nameswitch.co.uk

Resolution – family law with solicitors signed up to family-orientated code of practice: resolution.org.uk

Money and finances

Check your entitlement to state pension: gov.uk/check-state-pension

Conveyancing – Sail Legal: amicable.conveynext.co.uk/quote?

Lightning Reach – support for financial hardship: lightningreach.org/application-portal

National Debtline: nationaldebtline.org

Octopus Legacy – wills: octopuslegacy.com

Octopus Money coach: octopusmoney.com

Surviving Economic Abuse: survivingeconomicabuse.org

Turn2us – benefits support: turn2us.org.uk

Acknowledgements

There are so many people who have contributed to this book and who deserve my thanks. Rebecca Grey, of Profile Books, for spotting our Tube ad and being curious about the story behind it. The brilliant and patient freelance writing team, who have helped me put the book together: Emma Marriot, Patrick Taylor and Jan McCann.

My ever-patient agents, who've never knowingly rolled their eyes at the stream of very basic, first-time-author questions: Steph Thwaites and Sophie Lambert of Curtis Brown – joyous to work with, both! Also, to Leah Valaydon from Curtis Brown, who helped tirelessly with the back and forth of contractual points. My thanks, too, to Cindy Chan, publishing director at Souvenir Press – the lady who's kept the show on the road, ably assisted in that task by Georgina Difford of Profile Books, who has taught me publishing is a marathon not a sprint! Thank you to the marketing and publicity team at Profile Books: Dahmicca Wright and Kate McQuaid, as well as Mia Cameron for her help with the cover. Ali Nadal, for overseeing production, and the typesetter, Jonathan Baker, at Seagull Design.

Thank you to our pioneering customers, who simply want to show you there is a better way. Thank you to our investors, both those who, early on, backed us through our court case, and later, Octopus, who enabled us to reach more people. Special thanks to the amazing *amicable* team, who champion kinder separations with customers every single day and who are changing the narrative around divorce. Finally, special thanks are reserved for my friend (first and foremost – no mean feat after ten-plus years in business together) and co-founder, Pip Wilson: the kindest, brightest person I have ever met, and without whom none of this would have happened – you make me brave.

Index

ABC of separation 115–19
abusive relationships 32–3, 43, 87–8, 97, 133, 138, 163, 201
acceptance 37–8, 68, 71, 101, 104
actuary report 232, 240
adultery 18, 19, 30, 37
age statistics 21–2
AI chat bot 184
anger 39, 47, 62, 98–9, 112–13, 114, 163, 168, 171
apps 199
    co-parenting 159, 180–1, 193, 197
    dating 266, 267
arbitration 88–9
Atkins, Sue 168
attention, EAR technique 114

benefits 259
blended families 273–9
body language 117
'boiling frog metaphor' 41
business assets 233–4

calm tone 117
cash-flow modelling 242
child arrangements order 80, 156, 160–1
Child Maintenance Service (CMS) 192, 200–3, 204, 205
children 12–13, 32, 79–80, 85, 90, 105, 142–3, 151–206
    access 158, 277

after divorce 271–3
boundaries 176–80, 182, 276–7
child benefit 259
child maintenance 80, 140, 142–3, 159, 175, 191–205
co-parenting 12, 77, 110–11, 119, 133, 154–5, 159–63, 171, 176–87, 193, 206, 223, 250, 278
cooperative parenting 151–87
custody 18, 42, 158–9
finances 179, 189–206, 216
healthcare 174
holidays 173–4, 193, 262–3
house rules 175
living arrangements 172–3
nesting 53–4
no order principle 76
parallel parenting 163, 180–3
parental responsibility 157–8
parenting goals 172
parenting plan 76, 80, 82, 159, 161–2, 171–6, 178, 181, 182–3, 187, 199, 257, 272
poverty 202
reasons to stay 42
residency order 174
routines 254
school holidays 173

292

index

separation 51–5
special occasions 174
teenagers 156, 170–1, 183–7
telling 109, 163–70
travelling 237
see also education
Children Act 1989 157–8
Christmas 174
civil partnerships 20–1, 31, 33, 56, 75–6, 129
clean break order 80, 84, 140, 141–3, 150, 215
coercive control 32, 43
cohabitation 20, 23, 29, 33, 56, 57–8, 215
collaborative law process 86
Collect and Pay service 201, 202
common law partners 29
communication 77, 96–7, 101–8, 115, 123–4, 187, 198–9
'I want a divorce' 58–62
joint applications 132
conditional order 31, 78, 90, 141, 146, 257
conscious uncoupling 95
consent orders 11, 57–8, 76, 78–9, 80–4, 90, 136–43, 146–8, 150, 215–16, 235, 242–4, 257, 260
child maintenance 159, 192–205
D81 form 229–30
DIY agreements 81
mediation 82
Mesher order 142, 237–9
negotiation services 83
recital 204

wills 261
write-up services 84
see also financial order
contested proceedings 138
cooling-off period *see* reflection period
cooperation 96, 103, 112–14, 115, 123–4, 132
coping mechanisms 70–1
counselling 46, 47–8, 63, 67, 100, 180, 185, 253
courts 32, 87–8, 181
child maintenance 192
D81 form 229–30
financial disclosure 235
Form E 227–8

D81 form 229–30
dating
after divorce 264–73, 279
coach 267
decree absolute *see* final order
decree nisi *see* conditional order
deed polls 262
deed of separation *see* separation agreement
deemed or dispensed service 145
denial 39–40, 64, 98–9
desertion 30
divorce application 31, 56–7, 78, 128, 129–32, 137, 140, 142–3, 145
Divorce, Dissolution and Separation Act 2022 29–30, 128, 149
divorce petition *see* divorce application

do-it-yourself agreements 27, 77, 81–2
domicile 135
dos and don'ts checklist 122–3

EAR technique 113–15
Eddy, Bill 114
education 155, 156, 158, 174, 178–9, 181, 185
   no order principle 157
   school fees 143, 159, 194, 204
   school holidays 173
emotions
   emotional journey 9–10, 12, 38–40, 52, 60–2, 65, 67–8, 208
   emotional readiness 62–5, 98–104, 123
   money 207–8
empathy, EAR technique 114
employment after divorce 256
engagement rings 263–4
estate agents 231

family
   extended 179–80
   telling 108–12
family law 156–9
fault-based legal system 19, 30, 33, 128
fees 7–8
   consent orders 140
   contested proceedings 138
   divorce application 78, 130
   fixed 9, 83
'fight, flight, freeze or fawn?' 226

final order 31, 78–9, 141, 147–8, 250–4, 257, 262
finances 28, 76, 207–45
   after divorce 259–60
   cash-flow modelling 242
   child maintenance 80
   child's expenses 189–206
   clean break order 80, 84, 140, 141–3, 150, 215
   commitments 179
   disclosure 80, 81, 84, 141, 227–35
   earning capacity 217
   money coaching 214, 260
   reasons to stay 42
   remedy process 80
   separation 55, 56, 57
   spousal maintenance 217
   see also consent orders; pensions
financial order 137–43
   see also consent order
five-fault divorce system 19, 30, 31
foreign assets 229
foreign divorces 136
foreign marriages 129
foreign travel 262–3
Form A 230
Form E 6–7, 227–8
future claims 76, 79, 80, 84, 139, 140
future focus 84, 101, 114, 115–16, 124, 242

Gallimore, Candice 25
game theory 219–21

gender differences
    legal 18
    life expectancy 21–2
    remarriage 22
Gingerbread 202
goals 85
    after divorce 254–5
    GROW method 219, 222–6, 245
gratitude 255
grief 37, 38, 66, 69, 72, 168, 253
grounding techniques 117
GROW method 219, 222–45
guilt 24–5, 99, 121, 212, 284

habitual residence 134, 135
'help with fees application' 133
hobbies 256, 267
holidays 173–4, 193, 262–3
Horgan, Sharon 23–4
Huntingford, Paul 269–71

identity
    after divorce 255–6
    crisis 66

joint applications 79, 130–3, 145, 150
journalling 67
jurisdiction 134–5

kitchen-table agreements *see* do-it-yourself agreements
Koritzinsky, Allan R. 220
Kübler-Ross model 38–40

Langsford, Ruth 23

lawyers 4–9, 52, 85–6, 97, 104–6, 219, 223, 234–5
life expectancy 21–2
Lloyd, Rachael 266, 268
low income 130, 133

marital status 258–9
marriage
    certificate 129
    divorce rate 3, 20
    is it over? 37–72
    love 17–18
    moving out 52–3
    popularity 20
    possibilities for change 46
    reasons to stay 41–3
    remarriage 22, 139, 140–1
Martin, Chris 95
Matrimonial Causes Act 1923 18
Matrimonial Causes Act 1973 215
mediation 82–3, 84, 89, 138, 160, 180
Mediation Information and Assessment Meeting (MIAM) 138
Mesher order 142, 237–9
mindfulness 254
moving on 249–79

name changing 256, 258, 261–3
NameSwitch 262
negotiation services 83, 89–90
nesting 53–4
no-fault divorce 19, 29–32, 33, 127–8, 150
no order principle 76, 157, 160

Octopus Money 214, 232, 260
ownership 119, 121

Paltrow, Gwyneth 95
passports 173
patience 63–5, 71
pension on divorce experts (PODEs) 232
pensions 56, 76, 203, 217–18, 231–3, 239–42, 260
    attachment order 241
    CETV 232, 240
    offsetting 240–1
    sharing order 147–8, 240
Preece, James 267–8
property 28, 52–3, 56–7, 76, 80–1, 90, 138–9, 217, 223–4, 230–1, 236–9

reconciliation 57
Record of Agreement Form (RAF) 242
Red Book valuation 230–1
'red flag' behaviours 45
reflection period 31, 78, 90, 145–6, 149–50
religion 17, 23–4
remarriage 22, 139, 140–1
resilience 69
    children 155, 180
resistance 39–40, 98, 100, 119–22
respect 96, 103–4, 113–15, 123–4
Roseby, Paul 24, 69–71
routines 254
Royal Institution of Chartered Surveyors (RICS) 230
Rudkin, Angharad 155

safety 32, 268–9
same-sex couples 20, 24–5, 33, 69–71
self-care 67
self-soothing 67
separation 30, 50–8, 72
    ABC 115–19
    agreement 56–8
    legal 50, 51, 56–7
sleep problems 66, 253
social media 110–11
social stigma 18–19, 20, 23–4, 33, 41–2
sole applications 79, 130–3, 145, 150
solution focus 118
Split Happens 184
subscriptions 261
support 66, 100, 108, 179–80

tax relief 259
teenagers 156, 170–1
Thorne, Helen 257
time limits 119
timeline 145–7
Turn2us 259

unreasonable behaviour 30

Vince, Dale 143–4
visa 64, 65

Waldron, Kenneth H. 220
wedding rings 263–4
Wilde, Olivia 23
wills, updating 260–1
Winnicott, Donald W. 154
Wyatt, Kathleen 143–4